THE

ST. LOUIS CARDINALS FANS'
BUCKET LIST

DAN O'NEILL

TRIUMPH
B O O K S

Library of Congress Cataloging-in-Publication Data

Names: O'Neill, Dan, 1955–
Title: The St. Louis Cardinals fans' bucket list / Dan O'Neill.
Description: Chicago, Illinois : Triumph Books LLC, [2016] | Series: Bucket List
Identifiers: LCCN 2015043936 | ISBN 9781629371979
Subjects: LCSH: St. Louis Cardinals (Baseball team)—Miscellanea.
Classification: LCC GV875.S74 O64 2016 | DDC 796.357/640977866—dc23 LC record available at http://lccn.loc.gov/2015043936

This book is available in quantity at special discounts for your group or organization. For further information, contact:

Triumph Books LLC
814 North Franklin Street
Chicago, Illinois 60610
(312) 337-0747
www.triumphbooks.com

Printed in U.S.A.
ISBN: 978-1-62937-197-9
Design by Andy Hansen
Page production by Patricia Frey
Photos courtesy of AP Images unless otherwise noted

To my wife, Mary Pat, and my sons, Daniel, Riley, and Keegan, who fill my heart and complete my bucket list every day. And to my mom and dad, and all my brothers and sisters, who made growing up a fairy-tale adventure.

Contents

Foreword

The sun shining through the cracks in my bedroom window tells me that morning is here. I can almost feel the cool spring air through the panes. My alarm clock is set to go off in another hour, but there's no need...I'm wide awake.

There is a different vibe this morning that causes goose bumps to unexpectedly climb up and down my spine. I share a quick breakfast with my family, but my mind is somewhere else. Subconsciously, I am already locked on to the job at hand. Months and months of preparation have led me to this day.

My focus is sharper than normal. I hop in the truck and jump on the highway to head to work. Midway, I see the St. Louis Gateway Arch and it reminds me of where I am. As I pull off the exit, I can see thousands of people who have already begun placing their grills and banners and chairs out for the hours of tailgating ahead.

It's Opening Day in St. Louis, a recognized holiday here to everyone who is lucky enough to call it home. As I often do, just before I head through the gates, I look up at Busch Stadium with a sense of total awe.

This is where I get to work. Wow! As I head into the clubhouse, I see the pennants and the championship pictures and I smell the slight rankness in the air from past champagne celebrations.

All of this reminds me that I have a job to do and an organization to represent. Being a Cardinal is special, it's fun, it's important—and it's just plain cool.

If there's any doubt about any of that, the Clydesdales and the close to 50,000 strong in the sea of red that make up our daily attendance will serve as a reminder.

That's why I know Cardinals fans—those who live in St. Louis and those who follow from afar—will love checking the activities in this book off their bucket list. There are so many ways to show Cardinals pride in this city and elsewhere. Being a Cardinal is one of the best experiences a major league player might have. This book includes some of the best experiences one might have being a Cardinals fan.

—Adam Wainwright, 2015

Introduction

Baseball had a unique presence in my boyhood home. It was always there, in stacks of periodicals, newspapers, and issues of *Baseball Digest*. It was kept in big scrapbooks, chronicled in neatly trimmed articles, illustrated with black-and-white photos, and personalized by letters from former players and legendary scribes such as Fred Lieb and Dick Young.

Baseball came to life through the glowing tubes of a solid-state radio, encased in wood and garnished with a tall glass of Pepsi, extra ice. It cordoned off one corner of the living room, furnished with a small table, a porcelain lamp, and a reclining leather chair. It was nurtured and preserved there with Elmer's glue, paper clips, and a pair of scissors.

Sometimes it sounded like Radio Free Europe, strained by long distances, stressed by primitive technology, strangled by static interference. It arrived late at night, from places like New York, San Francisco, or Pittsburgh.

It was Morse code only my dad could decipher, unintelligible to most but music to his ears. He would listen intently—sitting in his chair, sipping his Pepsi, adjusting the dials, keeping score.

Baseball was about the Cardinals only in a begrudging sense, because it could no longer be about the Browns, the team he loved, the team that had left him in 1953. And ultimately, it wasn't about a single team as much as it was about passion.

Baseball was just a game in my house like *The Honeymooners* was just a show, like Kay Starr was just a singer, like a "bull-dogging headlock" was just a hold.

Baseball was a theology that sustained my father through a lifelong physical impairment, through several wars, through seven boys and two girls, through the rise and demise of the shoe business and his livelihood, and through my mother's chipped beef on toast.

My dad took me to games at the old ballpark at Grand and Dodier in St. Louis, but only if the Cardinals were playing one of his adopted teams, the Mets or Cubs. He also took me to semipro games at Heine Meine Field in south St. Louis. He knew who the players were...and he kept score.

Football? That was "the time between the end of the season and the start of spring training." Golf, fishing, and tennis? "The most boring activities in the world."

Baseball was bulletproof, noble and honest, something to preserve and protect. Baseball was the living gospel.

The game, and the Cardinals' relationship to it, has never been about "nation" building, wearing red, chasing squirrels, clapping to Clydesdales. Busch Stadium III isn't necessarily "baseball heaven," as they audaciously suggest before each Cardinals game. It's a ballpark, one of 30 in the major leagues.

At the National Baseball Hall of Fame induction ceremony in 1987, Ford C. Frick Award winner Jack Buck got up and waxed eloquently about his town. Buck said, "I don't want to be belligerent about it. But I kind of think, Mr. [George] Steinbrenner and others, that St. Louis is not only the heartland of America, but the best baseball city in the United States."

Buck was a beautiful man, speaking from the heart, representing his constituency. Ever since, St. Louisans have adopted that sentiment in a literal sense, as a national identity, a birthmark. The truth is there are a number of great baseball cities and great baseball fans around the country. It's not a quantitative measurement, not a Guinness entry.

St. Louis hasn't cornered the market on baseball allegiance. Sure, it's a nice idea, fun conversation, good marketing concept. After all, perception is reality. Say it often enough and people believe it. But if you have to tell someone what kind of baseball town you are, what kind of baseball town are you?

This isn't to suggest baseball isn't special in St. Louis—it is. But there is so much beneath the surface, so much more than popular trends, product proliferation, and self-promotion.

What can be said is that baseball is rich and vibrant in St. Louis, and the Cardinals are the coagulant. Organized ball has been played here for more than 150 years. It was a baseball village long before it opened a Ballpark Village, when the town ran north and south instead of east and west.

St. Louis had pennants before it had televisions, before it had airports. By the time baseball arrived in Arlington, Texas, St. Louis had been to the World Series 12 times. In October 1944, St. Louis had two teams in a World Series that was played entirely at one ballpark. Travel-weary baseball writers get goose bumps when they read that.

Baseball hasn't always been the clean, decorous, symmetrical package it is now. It was gritty, quirky, even awkward at times. It was choked with bus exhaust and cluttered with pavement-pounding streetcars. It was segregated by color; filtered by right-field screens and limited views; embellished by Dixieland bands, "Mighty Wurlitzer" organs, and manual scoreboards.

It smelled like popcorn and cheap cigars. It felt like sticky concrete and wooden chairs. It sounded like exploding paper cups. It was a neighborhood joint, not an entertainment complex.

In the interest of full disclosure, I didn't play a lot of organized baseball growing up. I spent many more summer days immersed in the adjunct applications: Indian Ball, Fuzzball, Corkball, Hot Box, and Wiffle Ball. The game of choice was dictated by the number of kids in attendance.

Depending on the circumstances, identities were assumed and shared. Musial one day, Boyer the next. Flood for chasing flies, Maxvill for grounders, Gagliano for grins.

We had the avatars down pat: how they walked, how they stood, how they dug in. We knew their swing, their windup, and their trot. We knew the subtle artistry of the hook slide, the purpose of the crow hop, the timing of the drag bunt. We knew them like we knew our way home.

We could flick our wrists like Henry Aaron, basket catch like Willie Mays, stretch like Bill White. Baseball's biggest selling point was what we had in spades—imagination.

Inspiration is easy to find in St. Louis; reference points are abundant. As of early 2016, the last National League pitcher to win 30 games was a Cardinal. The last National League player to win a Triple Crown was a Cardinal. The last right-handed batter to hit .400 was a Cardinal. The last player to steal 100 bases in a season was a Cardinal. The last kid to grow up in St. Louis and hit a World Series home run off Whitey Ford was a Cardinal. Get up, Mike Shannon, get up!

The last American sports figure to be a genuine role model was a Cardinal. And Stan "the Man" Musial might hold that title for some time to come.

But it's even more than that. It's DNA that is crossgenerational, a gene that lies dormant deep inside until triggered, unsolicited and inexplicably. For St. Louisans, baseball is like a song that takes you back, to another time, another place, another experience.

It's there in one of Buck's calls, one of Brock's slides, one of Ozzie's flips. It might be one word, one thought, one "Freese" frame.

We retain that gene for God knows what reason. It means something different to each of us. And it means the same to all of us, an association that comes in a kaleidoscope of colors and characters, imprinted in our brains. It is Ed Spiezio's spring, Mike Laga's foul ball, Ted Simmons' hair, Orlando Cepeda's limp, Scipio Spinks' gorilla, Jim Lindeman's luck.

The names are rhythmic: Pepper Martin, Carl Sawatski, and Wilmer "Vinegar Bend" Mizell. The movements are poetic, like Jim Edmonds diving, Jack Clark ripping, or Ken Reitz Zamboni-ing. The snapshots can be stunning, like Roger Freed's grand slam, Ray Washburn's no-hitter, and Glenn Brummer's steal of home. The heroes are improbable, like Barney Schultz, Tom Lawless, and Jeff Weaver.

Baseball is what separates us from the animals in St. Louis. We identify with high schools, we love toasted ravioli, and we trust in only one true prophet—Whitey Herzog.

Along with the Rexall drugstore, vanilla phosphates, and Christmas mornings, baseball is what I miss about being a kid. It's why I became a sportswriter, why my wardrobe is so limited, and why, as I compiled this book, I couldn't help but feel closer to "the Skipper."

His bucket list would look quite a bit different than this one. But it would have the same passion, inspiration, and vocation. It would be about absorbing all there is to absorb from a storied franchise and the greatest game.

Sorry this couldn't be about the Browns, Dad. But I couldn't have done it without you.

Chapter 1

Things to Do

Throw Out the First Pitch at a Cardinals Game

WHERE: The pitching mound, Busch Stadium, 700 Clark Avenue, St. Louis, MO 63102. Go to the Cardinals' website at http://stlouis .cardinals.mlb.com/stl/fan_forum/attpitch/index.jspb and enter a contest to be selected.

WHEN: Before a Cardinals game

WHAT TO DO: Throw a baseball 60'6"…or less

COST: If you're 50 Cent, Carl Lewis, Carly Rae Jepsen, or Mariah Carey…public humiliation. But if you can throw a ball, nothing.

BUCKET RANK: 🪣🪣🪣

. . . .

At some point in their lives, just about everyone has wondered what it might be like to throw out the first pitch at a ballgame. Technically speaking, the Cardinals still have a "first pitch" before every home game. But they also have a second pitch, third pitch, fourth pitch…a number of ceremonial pitches.

The designated Cardinals player who has the duty of catching the "first pitch," usually an unheralded rookie, might wind up catching three innings some nights. Okay, I'm exaggerating, but you get the point. In fact, stadium operations has come to officially reference the activity as throwing out a "ceremonial pitch" rather than a first pitch.

This privilege used to be strictly reserved for politicians, Hollywood celebrities, distinguished alumni, those types. You may recall President Barack Obama throwing out the first pitch to Cardinals All-Star Albert Pujols before the 2009 All-Star Game at Busch Stadium III in St. Louis. The president wore a black Chicago White Sox jacket, which was genuine on his part, but not particularly popular with the sea of red that night.

Five years earlier, President George W. Bush did it right. Bush wore a Cardinals-red jacket when he became the first to throw the presidential Opening Day pitch in St. Louis. He fired a strike to Cardinals catcher Mike Matheny and later told broadcaster Mike Shannon, "I've done a lot of exciting things since I've been the president, but standing out here in Busch Stadium is one of the exciting ones."

Hail to the chief!

The concept of the first pitch actually started when Prime Minister Okuma Shigenobu made a ceremonial toss before a Japanese League game in Koshien, Japan, in 1908. Two years later, U.S. President William Howard Taft started the tradition in America, celebrating Opening Day at Washington's Griffith Stadium in 1910.

Since the Taft toss, every president has thrown a baseball as part of the fun at a major league park, be it at Opening Day, the All-Star Game, or the World Series. Warren Harding is generally considered one of the worst presidents in history. But he was a real baseball fan, so he had that going for him...which was nice.

Harding liked throwing out first pitches so much, he threw two of them in 1923—one at Yankee Stadium and one at Griffith Stadium two days later. If he was first-pitching today, Harding would probably go on the disabled list after all of that, and eventually be a candidate for Tommy John surgery.

To start, the ceremonial pitch ritual featured the honored guest tossing a ball to a player or coach from his seat in the stands. Some may recall Cardinals owner August A. "Gussie" Busch doing so from his owner's box beside the dugout on occasion.

However, President Ronald Reagan altered the playing field when he insisted on making a ceremonial pitch from in front of the mound before a Baltimore Orioles game at Memorial Stadium in 1984. President Bill Clinton went a few steps farther in 1993, throwing a first pitch from the mound at Camden Yards. He was the first president to actually toe the slab.

The first pitch can be heartwarming as well as ceremonial. For instance, in May 2015, 106-year-old Arnold Vouga was among those making a ceremonial pitch at Busch Stadium. A lifelong fan, Vouga recalled attending Game 4 of the 1926 World Series between the Cardinals and Yankees at Sportsman's Park. Babe Ruth hit three home runs that day, the last of which left the park and crashed through a window of the auto dealership on the opposite side of Grand Avenue.

Vouga said he once bumped into Stan Musial at a drug store and the Cardinals star was buying cigars. "I told him those weren't very good for him," Vouga said. "And he told me, 'Yeah, but they sure taste good.'"

From presidents to faithful fans, it has reached the point where anyone might have the opportunity to throw out a ceremonial first pitch. Celebrities are still in the mix, but so are corporate sponsors, winners of charity auctions, those who have performed community service, those who have served in the military, and others.

The Cardinals also conduct the AT&T Make Your Pitch Sweepstakes, in which fans can win the opportunity to take the mound, as well as tickets to a game. You go to the Cardinals' website, make a written pitch as to why you should be selected, and hope for the best.

For example, one Make Your Pitch offering from Larry in St. Charles, Missouri, went like this:

"I've always wanted to throw out the first pitch. To have thousands of people cheer for me as I win the World Series has been a dream since I was a child."

Dear Larry, you might be a little confused. See, having thousands cheer for you as you win the World Series is not the first pitch, it's the last pitch. Baseball hasn't made that a ceremonial function or sponsored event just yet. But hang in there, it might be coming.

- -

Frame the Classic 1968 Sports Illustrated Magazine Cover

There have been a lot of terrific *Sports Illustrated* covers featuring Cardinals players over the years. Certainly, the January 24, 2013, regional issue of the magazine, which honored the life of Stan Musial by printing four consecutive covers in its pages, is a gem. Musial appeared on the cover of the magazine eight times.

But perhaps the most notable—or notorious—*SI* cover concerning the Cardinals was the October 7, 1968, edition that featured the "World Champion St. Louis Cardinals" dressed in street clothes and seated in front of their Busch Stadium II cubicles, with their uniform jerseys hanging alongside.

The cover was actually a fold, necessary to get all of the players and the manager, Red Schoendienst, into the frame. On the inside fold of the image there was a headline and graphic: "The Highest-Paid Team in Baseball History."

The partial cover image featured Roger Maris, Tim McCarver, Bob Gibson, Mike Shannon, and Lou Brock. The unfolded image included Orlando Cepeda, Curt Flood, Julian Javier, and Dal Maxvill, as well as manager Schoendienst, seated alongside in his Cardinals garb, holding his cap.

The image is striking, revealing a group of fashionably dressed, confident, young, successful men—black, white, and Hispanic—a world-champion baseball team unplugged. The graphic also tells a story about how times have changed.

Keep in mind, this cover came out exactly one year to the day before Flood was traded to the Philadelphia Phillies: October 7, 1969. The Cardinals center fielder refused to report and challenged baseball's reserve clause. He lost, but Flood's actions opened the door to baseball free agency and eventually changed the economics of sports.

So what did these world-champion, extravagantly paid, 1968 Cardinals make? The graphic lays it out:

Maris: $75,000

McCarver: $60,000

Gibson: $85,000

Shannon: $40,000

Brock: $70,000

Cepeda: $80,000

Flood: $72,500

Javier: $45,000

Maxvill: $37,500

Schoendienst: $42,000

Add it all up, and the "highest-paid team in baseball history" made $607,000, or $1 million less than Cardinals reserve outfielder Peter Bourjos, who collected $1,650,000 in 2015. The major league minimum was $507,500.

But there is one more thing especially compelling about the 1968 cover: the events it appeared to set into motion. No doubt you have heard of the *Sports Illustrated* cover jinx, which suggests any players or team that appear on the magazine cover are doomed to misfortune.

Urban legend? You be the judge, and consider what took place when that *SI* cover hit the newsstands—which still existed in 1968.

The day before the magazine officially came out—October 6—the NL-champion Cardinals demolished the Detroit Tigers 10–1 to take a 3–1 lead in the World Series. At that point, the "El Birdos" appeared to be a lock for their second consecutive world championship.

Gibson, who struck out a record 17 Tigers in the opening game, struck out 10 more in Game 4 and beat 31-game winner Denny McLain for the second time. At that point, Gibson had won seven consecutive World Series starts. With his record regular season earned run average of 1.12, he seemed untouchable.

Also in Game 4, Lou Brock pounded his second homer of the Series, to go with a double, a triple, four runs batted in, and his seventh stolen base in four games. At that point, Brock was batting .500.

As a team, the Cardinals banged out 13 hits, seven of them for extra bases. They were rolling.

On October 7, 1968, the magazine officially came out. That same day, the Cardinals lost Game 5 under strange circumstances. It was a game they led 3–0 after the first inning—and still led 3–2 in the top of the fifth when Brock doubled and Javier singled to left.

Normally a defensive liability, burly Detroit outfielder Willie Horton uncorked a strong throw to the plate that was right on the money. The speedy Brock, the game's premier base runner, inexplicably elected to arrive standing up rather than sliding. He was ruled out on catcher Bill Freehan's quick tag. The inning and the momentum died. The Tigers rallied and won 5–3.

Back at Busch Stadium, hoping to close out the series at home on October 9, the Cardinals managed just one run off McLain in Game 6 and were blasted 13–1. The Series was tied 3–3.

Still, no reason for Cardinals fans to worry. The reigning champions had the home field for Game 7 and they had Gibson in the green

SPORTS ILLUSTRATED COVER

O n May 27, 2013, *Sports Illustrated* re-created the cover it did in 1968 with a slightly different twist. The Cardinals' starting pitching staff is shown seated in front of their cubicles, and the headline is "The Cardinal Way," an expression adopted by team enthusiasts and generally despised by opposing parties.

As an alternative, or complement, to the 1968 version, the 2013 cover is much easier to acquire. Unlike the '68 cover, the May 27, 2013, "Cardinal Way" cover is offered on the www.sicovers.com website and can be purchased for $19.95 before shipping.

In the cover story, *SI* writer Ben Reiter explained why it made sense to put the Cardinals on the cover and recreate the special image from 45 years earlier.

"When we think of the Cardinals, we think of a distinct organizational culture: Anodyne, diligent, supportive, resolute," wrote Reiter. "Mostly, we think of consistency. Their 11 championships have been well distributed. No son or daughter of St. Louis born since 1902 has reached the age of 25 without having lived through at least one victory parade."

The graphic that went along with the photo had nothing to do with salaries. This time it was about the club's starting rotation. It also reflected the advance time involved in committing to a cover photo and story. It read:

"ARCH SUPPORT: Adam Wainwright, Shelby Miller, Jaime Garcia, Lance Lynn, and Jake Westbrook turn MLB's best rotation—and St. Louis' depth ensures the staff won't skip a beat even with Garcia and Westbrook injured."

What you have here is a rare case of the *SI* jinx actually going into effect at the time of conception. Obviously, the magazine shot the photo and planned the story shortly before finding out Garcia and Westbrook were lost to injuries. In too deep to pull out at that point, the editors chose the option of running the qualifying sentiment in the graphics, covering their tracks.

That's not where the bewitching ends. That 2013 Cardinals team finished with the exact same record as its 1968 cover predecessor, 97–65. It also lost in the World Series, falling in six games to the Boston Red Sox.

From that *SI* cover group, Garcia made only nine starts before missing the rest of the 2013 season with nerve damage in his pitching elbow. He did not appear in the postseason, missed most of 2014, and missed a large chunk of 2015, as well.

Westbrook finished 7–8 with a 4.63 earned run average in 2013. He did not appear in the postseason and was out of baseball altogether by 2014. Miller went 15–9 in 2013 but didn't pitch in the postseason past the division series. In November 2014, Miller was traded with prospect Tyrell Jenkins to the Atlanta Braves in a deal that brought outfielder Jason Heyward and reliever Jordan Walden.

Wainwright, clearly identified in the picture as the leader of the pack, had a terrific regular 2013 season, finishing 19–9. But after going 2–0 in a division series win over Pittsburgh, the right-hander's luck went south.

He was 0–1 in the NLCS and 0–2 with a 4.50 ERA in the World Series. Lynn was 15–10 with a 3.97 ERA during the '13 season, 0–1 with a 4.76 ERA in the Fall Classic.

In fact, the Cardinals' best pitcher when the postseason push came to shove was someone *not* pictured on the *SI* cover—rookie Michael Wacha.

Wacha was 4–1 with a 2.78 ERA down the regular season stretch for the Cardinals. His performance was so impressive it kicked Miller to the postseason sidelines. Wacha flirted with a no-hitter while beating the

Pirates in the division series. He went 2–0 with a 0.00 ERA against the Dodgers in the NLCS. He beat the Red Sox 4–2 in Game 2 to get the Cardinals even in the World Series.

Wacha finally showed he was human, succumbing to the Red Sox and a hostile Fenway Park in Game 6, but the message is clear: if you want to be successful in sports, stay off the cover of *Sports Illustrated*.

room. Gibson had won back-to-back Game 7s (1964 and 1967), pitched seven consecutive World Series complete game victories, dominated the Tigers in two previous games, and dominated all of baseball with a 1.12 earned run average, and would be named the National League's MVP and Cy Young Award winner after the season.

How could the Cardinals lose, right? They did.

They did because Brock—featured on the cover of the April 15, 1968, *Sports Illustrated*—was picked off first base in the bottom of the sixth. After the October 7 edition came out, Brock had no more steals, committed an error, and was thrown out on the base paths three times over the last three games.

They did because Flood—featured on an August 19, 1968, cover of *Sports Illustrated* as "baseball's best center fielder"—misplayed Jim Northrup's seventh-inning drive into a two-run triple. Flood was also picked off base in the sixth inning.

They did because the only run they mustered off Detroit left-hander Mickey Lolich was Shannon's two-out homer in the ninth.

They lost 4–1.

The "highest-paid team in baseball history" lost three straight, including Game 7 on October 10, 1968, after the *SI* cover came out. Not saying the jinx is real or anything, but....

Thanks a lot, *Sports Illustrated*.

Name a Child or Pet "Vinegar Bend"

In the annals of baseball, there have been some unforgettable names—William Van Winkle "Chicken" Wolf, Urban Shocker, Coco Crisp, Dennis "Oil Can" Boyd, Razor Shines, Choo Choo Coleman, and Chief Bender, to offer just a small sampling.

And the Cardinals have had their share of interesting names, from Mordecai "Three Finger" Brown, to Dizzy Dean, to Stubby Clapp. But when it comes to memorable names, it's hard to top David Wilmer "Vinegar Bend" Mizell.

There's nothing particularly mysterious about the name. Mizell was born on Aug. 13, 1930, and his place of birth is listed as Vinegar Bend, Alabama. Hence the nickname.

The township of Vinegar Bend is located in the far southwest corner of the state, part of Washington County, some 15 miles southwest of Chatom. As of 2014, Vinegar Bend had a population of 196 and an average household income of $46,951.

The town occupies just a bit more than nine miles of Alabama real estate and used to have a ZIP code of 36584. But when the bridge on the main road into Vinegar Bend was closed for repairs, the U.S. Post Office there closed for good.

Vinegar Bend got its name when a train passing through the area careened off the tracks and spilled its load of vinegar there.

The funny thing is, Mizell was not actually born in Vinegar Bend and never actually lived in the town. He was born across the state line in Mississippi. But the family's residence was on the Vinegar Bend,

Alabama, mail route, so his birthplace was recorded as being Vinegar Bend.

Wilmer Mizell was raised by his grandmother and uncle and went to high school in Leakesville, Mississippi. His father died when he was just two years old and his mother became ill shortly thereafter.

As a baseball player, he was the stereotypical, hard-throwing kid, straight off the farm. When he was 17, Mizell attended a Cardinals tryout camp in Biloxi, Mississippi, and struck out the only three batters he faced. A short while later, scout Bobby Lewis signed the young left-hander to a contract.

As hard as he threw, Mizell had problems with control and holding runners on base early in his career. His first professional pitch for Class D Albany sailed 20 feet over the backstop.

But Mizell settled down to go 12–3 with a 1.98 ERA for Albany, striking out 175 batters in 141 innings. In 1950, Mizell pitched Class B Winston-Salem to the Carolina League title by compiling a 17–7 mark with a team-leading 2.48 ERA. The following season, he moved up to Houston and led the Texas League with 257 strikeouts in 238 innings. In a game against Dallas, he fanned 18 batters, tying the league record.

Along the way, his farm-boy upbringing and rustic charm became the stuff of which promotional dreams are made. At Winston-Salem, Mizell rode around the field one night on a mule and then sang country music over the public-address system.

"I walked behind more mules than I walked batters, and that's saying a lot," he said of his country beginnings.

While he was pitching for Houston in '51, the club held a "Vinegar Bend Night" promotion and brought in 32 people from Vinegar Bend, supposedly representing the entire adult population of the town.

Mizell suggested Vinegar Bend was so small, some of the honored guests "must've come from the suburbs." He also struck out 15 Shreveport batters that night.

In 1952, Mizell came to the Cardinals' big-league camp. Sportswriter Red Smith watched his blazing fastball and unorthodox motion and called him a "left-handed Dizzy Dean." But the 6'3" Mizell never quite reached those Hall of Fame heights.

Still, his raw talent continued to intrigue and he produced moments of brilliance. In his rookie season in 1952, he finished 10–8 and struck out 146 in 190 innings. He also led the National League with 103 walks. The following season, Mizell went 13–11 with a 3.49 earned run average and 173 strikeouts in 224.1 innings.

Shortly after the 1953 season ended, at the age of 23, his career took a detour. He was inducted into the Army and spent the next two summers in the service. When Mizell returned, he went 14–14 for a 1956 Cardinals team that finished 76–78. He won 13 games for the seventh-place Cardinals in 1959 and was selected to the All-Star Game. Back problems forced him to miss the opportunity.

When 1960 began, the Cardinals were in need of a second baseman and Mizell got off to a rough start. In late May, the popular lefty was traded to Pittsburgh, along with infielder Dick Gray, for second baseman Julian Javier and pitcher Ed Bauta.

That summer became the highlight of Mizell's career, as he was a key contributor to a world-championship run for the Bucs. In 23 starts for Pittsburgh, Mizell went 13–5 with a 3.12 ERA. He hurled three shutouts, including a 1–0 three-hitter at Cincinnati on September 18, and had one stretch of 30 consecutive scoreless innings. The Pirates won the pennant and famously beat the Yankees on Bill Mazeroski's home run.

Former Cardinals teammate Ken Boyer once described what it was like to face Mizell and his exaggerated delivery. "The guy shows you his glove, shows you his rear, and somebody tells you it's a strike," Boyer said.

Mizell's performance in Pittsburgh dropped off in 1961, as he continued to lose velocity on his once-vaunted fastball. He was traded to the New York Mets in May 1962 and was out of baseball entirely by 1963, at the age of 32.

When his baseball career ended, Mizell became a member of the 91st United States Congress in 1968, a Republican representing North Carolina for three terms. He would go on to hold administrative posts for three different presidents, including Gerald Ford, Ronald Reagan, and George H.W. Bush. When he retired, he resided in Midway, North Carolina.

And he never completely lost his stuff. In an annual Congressional baseball game, he once struck out seven Democrats in succession, causing the opposing manager to threaten, "'If this guy throws one more pitch, we walk off the field.'"

Mizell never became the 20-game winner the Cardinals envisioned, but he finished 90–88 with a 3.85 ERA in nine major league seasons. And he put the town of Vinegar Bend on the map as one of baseball's most memorable names.

"The worst thing that happened to us back home in Vinegar Bend was the time we had the fire," Mizell once recalled. "It started in the bathroom. Fortunately, we were able to put it out before it reached the house."

Mizell died at the age of 68 while visiting his wife's family in Kerrville, Texas. He was survived by two sons, Danny and Dave, who both lived in North Carolina, and by four grandchildren.

To this day, none of the immediate Mizell family has lived in Vinegar Bend.

Play St. Louis Cardinals Monopoly

What better combination is there than an iconic board game and an iconic baseball franchise, brought together by six pewter figures, a pair of dice, and a "Get Out of Jail Free" card?

Most of us have played Monopoly at some point in our lives, as excited children or extremely bored adults. In 2015, the game celebrated its 80th anniversary.

And the concept is actually older, born in 1903 by anti-monopolist Elizabeth (Lizzie) J. Magie Phillips. She was trying to explain the single-tax theory of political economist Henry George through an adventurous board game. She intended the exercise to be educational and called it "The Landlord's Game."

In 1935, Parker Brothers—no relation to former Cardinals pitcher Harry Parker—introduced Monopoly, with the familiar 4×10 space-to-a-side design of the layout and the "Chance" and "Community Chest" cards. The original Monopoly was based on streets in Atlantic City, New Jersey. The notion the game was invented solely by Charles Darrow is false. But that wives' tale became so popular that by the 1970s, Darrow was credited in the instructions.

Those were dark days for Monopoly. Let's call them the steroid era.

More recently, Hasbro succeeded Parker Brothers as the parent producers, and the game has undergone a number of redesigns and alterations. Some form of Monopoly has been licensed in 103 countries and printed in 37 languages. Most are in the original format, with street names replaced with locales from a particular town, university, or fictional place.

But a number of sports-related versions of the game have been marketed as well, representing Olympic, FIFA soccer, NFL, NHL, and MLB teams.

The first of the two Cardinals games came out in 2001, perhaps as a delayed reaction to Mark McGwire's home run chase of 1998. McGwire was still with the Cardinals in '01, although his production dropped from 70 homers in '98 to an injury-slowed 29 homers three years later. He would call it quits at the end of the season.

It is also interesting to note that Mike Matheny, current Cardinals manager, was the catcher on the Tony La Russa–managed '01 club. The middle of the lineup was still fortified by Albert Pujols and Jim Edmonds. Pitcher Matt Morris enjoyed his best season in 2001, finishing 22–8, while Darryl Kile won 16 games. The following season, Kile would be discovered dead in his hotel room during a series in Chicago, a difficult chapter in Cardinals history.

The 2001 Cardinals won 93 games, but they couldn't get past Randy Johnson, Curt Schilling, and the Arizona Diamondbacks in the National League Division Series. They lost 2–1 in a decisive Game 5 when Arizona's Tony Womack's reached Steve Kline for a two-out single in the ninth.

But the 2001 version of Cardinals Monopoly is more about the history of the franchise than a particular team. You compete to own some of the Cardinals' greatest assets, including the 1926 World Series Championship; Hall of Fame players like Dizzy Dean, Rogers Hornsby, and Johnny Mize; and 2001 standouts like Matt Morris, Edgar Renteria, or Ray Lankford.

This collector's edition attempts to bring the Cardinals and old Busch Memorial Stadium to life with classic moments in franchise history.

In the 2006 World Series edition, Pujols and Edmonds are still prominent members of the team and Tony La Russa is still the skipper. What is not reflected is that the 2001 team—though it fell short of a world championship—was probably better than the 2006 version.

The '06 Cardinals won only 83 regular season games—the fewest regular-season wins ever by a World Series champion a full season. Statistically speaking, it is the worst team ever to become world champions.

But that Cardinals club caught fire in the postseason, boosted by a number of dramatic events and unlikely heroes. Some of those episodes, including Yadier Molina's game-winning home run and Adam Wainwright's strikeout of Mets outfielder Carlos Beltran in Game 7 of the National League Championship Series, are immortalized by Monopoly.

What's more, you can buy, sell, and trade players, taking risks and making decisions as you build your own championship club, in a Monopoly sort of way. Remember, hindsight *is* 20/20. So, given Pujols would later leave the organization to sign a free-agent deal with the Angels, given Encarnacion would suffer a career-ending injury in 2007, given Spiezio would have substance-abuse problems the following year and Mark Mulder would never win another big-league game, you might want to move all of them while you have a chance in 2006.

Just sayin'.

By the way, in the 2006 version those cute little pewter figures include batter, pitcher, catcher's mask, hot dog, baseball in glove, and the World Series Trophy. The game is projected to take 120 minutes to play, but offers a 60-minute option to make things go faster. That said, obviously, there is no instant replay. The '06 version also comes with one of five limited-edition trading cards, which include McGwire, Edmonds, Kile, Lankford, and Renteria.

Play ball!

Roll the Dice on "First Pitch" Tickets

WHERE: Busch Stadium, 700 Clark Avenue, St. Louis, MO 63102, Gate 3 on west side of stadium

WHEN: First Pitch Ticket sales begin at 9:00 AM on the day of a game and promise to stay open until two hours before the game or until all the tickets are gone

WHAT TO DO: Purchase a voucher for a pair of tickets to that day's or evening's game

COST: $11.20

BUCKET RANK: 🪣

The Cardinals offer a unique First Pitch Tickets program that is sponsored by their flagship radio station, 1120 AM KMOX.

If you have the time, and an adventurous heart, it is a cheap and fun way to acquire tickets. Every game day during the regular season, the first 275 fans at Busch Stadium's 8th Street ticket window located near Gate 3 have the opportunity to acquire a pair of tickets to that day's or evening's game for just $11.20. That's right: two ticks, $11.20.

The best part—or worst part, if you will—is that where those seats will be located is anybody's guess. There is a catch—you have to be at the right place at the right time. First Pitch Ticket sales begin at 9:00 AM on the day of a game and promise to stay open until two hours before the game or until all the tickets are gone, whichever comes first.

Take a guess at which normally happens first. That's right: those 550 seats don't last long. The paying customers are given a voucher that entitles them to two tickets for $11.20. The buyer will be required to show a picture ID at the time of purchase.

Once the voucher is secured, the fun begins. The pool of First Pitch seats are taken from various locations: tickets returned to the office by Cardinals players, the visiting club, sponsors, groups, and others. The tickets can be anywhere in the ballpark, from Field Level box seats, to Terrace, to Standing Room Only.

Ten minutes before the game, those holding a voucher are asked to produce it, along with a picture ID, and claim their prize at the "First Pitch Tickets" sign located at Gate 1. The treasured ducats will be distributed on a random basis, handed to them in sealed envelopes. Exchanges will not be permitted. In short, it's kind of like being on *Let's Make a Deal* and waiting to see what's behind door No. 1.

All that money you saved on purchasing the seats can now be spent on gorging at the concessions. There is one qualification. First Pitch Tickets fans are not guaranteed to receive any promotional items that are given away at the gates.

So, a word to the wise. If you were going to the game specifically to add to your bobblehead collection, or if you are there to actually throw out a ceremonial first pitch, you may want to pursue other means of entering the stadium.

Attend Cardinals Fantasy Camp

WHERE: Two options: 700 Clark Avenue, St. Louis, MO 63102; Roger Dean Stadium, 4751 Main Street, Jupiter, FL 33458

WHEN: The Roger Dean Stadium version is conducted in January. The Busch Stadium edition is held in June.

WHAT TO DO: Call the Cardinals' offices at (314) 345-9000 and ask for information, or email fantasycamp@cardinals.com.

COST: The camps cost anywhere from $5,495 to $7,500, depending on which camp you attend, the package you choose, and your status (rookie or returning camper). A deposit of $900 is required to reserve a spot on the roster. The balance must be paid no later than October 1.

BUCKET RANK: 🪣🪣🪣🪣

We've all done it since we were kids, since we first stepped into a real baseball stadium and saw the perfect green grass and milky-white uniforms. We've all imagined being there, stepping to the plate, the bases loaded, getting the walk-off hit...racing into the gap to make a diving catch...blowing a fastball past a villainous hitter...being mobbed by teammates, hearing the cheers, living the dream.

The good news is, once you reach an age where the dream is no longer even remotely possible, you can live it...sort of.

Since 2000, the Cardinals have been conducting fantasy camps in which frustrated big leaguers 27 years of age or older have the chance to wear the Birds on the Bat and rub elbows with the guys who have done it for real.

In 2015, two such camps were held in January at the club's spring training home, Roger Dean Stadium in Jupiter, Florida. The first gathering was five days long, the second was three days. Another camp, even more realistic, was conducted in June over four days at Busch Stadium.

"The Busch Stadium Fantasy Camp experience is like no other in sports," said Joe Pfeiffer, Cardinals Fantasy Camp Director. "Campers get to suit up in a personalized uniform at their own locker, select walk-up music, and play baseball on the Busch Stadium field alongside living legends; it doesn't get much better."

Actually, it *does* get much better. It's much better to be 25 years old or younger and be paid David Price's salary of $30 million per summer to do those things. But short of that, yes, the fantasy camps give you a dose of what it's like to be in "the Show," as they like to say. And as long as you don't get too realistic, pull a "hammy," and go on the 15-day disabled list, it's great fun.

Campers dress in their own, personalized uniforms at their own cubicles—albeit in the visitors' locker room at Busch Stadium. They receive instruction from the likes of longtime Cardinals coach Jose Oquendo and play four seven-inning games over the four days on the sacred turf at Busch. Two former Cardinals players are among their teammates, and a former Cardinals player or manager serves as their skipper.

In 2015, the Cardinals alumni attending the camp in one capacity or another included Herzog, Sutter, Brock, McGee, Andy Benes, Dave LaPoint, Rick Horton, Brian Jordan, Todd Worrell, Scott Cooper, Ted Savage, Gary Bennett, Rick Ankiel, Kyle McClellan, Jason Isringhausen, and Scott Terry.

Horton, a former Cardinals pitcher and current broadcaster, said he gets as much out of the experience as the campers.

"It's good for my soul," he explained. "I've loved baseball my whole life and I get a chance to love it with campers who are almost going back to their youth a little bit. It's not about performance but it's about the joy of being connected through baseball."

Perks include special autograph and photo sessions, party-suite tickets to a Cardinals game to kick off the camp, and two special dinners. The first dinner in 2015 included a Hall of Fame chat with Brock and Sutter. The following night, the Cardinals celebrated the 30th anniversary of their 1985 National League pennant–winning team with Whitey Herzog, McGee Horton, and Vince Coleman holding court.

The camps at Roger Dean also included a "So You Think You Can Hit a Big-Leaguer?" contest where campers got a chance to see what it's like to face a major league pitcher.

Campers pay a healthy price for all of this big-league treatment. The cost for the camps ranges from $5,500 to $7,500, and that does not include airfare. Here is the breakdown for the 2015 camps.

Roger Dean Stadium Camps
First-time camper $6,000/Returning camper $5,500

- 5 days/4 nights single-room accommodations at the Marriott Palm Beach Gardens

- Daily transportation provided to/from Roger Dean Stadium

- Breakfast and lunch provided daily in the St. Louis Cardinals Spring Training Clubhouse

- Evening festivities (Opening Reception, Talkin' Baseball, Awards Banquet, Closing Picnic).

- Cardinals apparel provided: home white uniform—authentic jersey and pants; red batting-practice jersey; authentic Cardinals sweatshirt, belt, socks, and hat (you must provide your own glove, rubber cleats, and other personal items)

- Instruction and coaching from the St. Louis Cardinals Legends

- Daily games against other campers (seven games minimum)

- One five-inning game against a full St. Louis Cardinals Legends team

- A "Camp Reunion" with All-Inclusive Suite tickets to a 2015 regular season Cardinals game (TBD)

- 8x10 photo with the St. Louis Cardinals Legends.

- Access to all training and practice facilities at Roger Dean Stadium Complex

- Use of St. Louis Cardinals Clubhouse staff and athletic trainers

- Airfare NOT included

MVP Package
First-timers $7,500/ Returning camper $7,000

Includes all of the above plus…

- Private instructional session with the Cardinal Legends and Hall of Fame Players

- Private Meet & Greet luncheon with the Hall of Fame Players on Wednesday

- Two additional items for autograph signing session, provided by the Cardinals

- Event/camp-long recognition as an MVP Camper

- Pregame, on-field ceremony/recognition at the "Camp Reunion" Cardinals game

- Personalized Fantasy Camp bat

Busch Stadium Fantasy Camp
First-time camper $5,995/Returning camper $5,495

- Four teams (44 roster spots for campers)

- Receive authentic Majestic Cardinals uniform (two jerseys/white pants) and two authentic New Era Cardinals hats

- Dress at customized locker in visiting-team clubhouse at Busch Stadium

- Two party-suite tickets for camp opening reception and game

- Memorabilia items for autographs from Hall of Fame Players

- Two special dinner events including Hall of Fame Players such as Whitey Herzog, Bruce Sutter, Lou Brock, and other former Cardinals

• •

The Redbird Express is an inexpensive, convenient, and safe way to get to and from a Cardinals game. In 1996, the shuttle bus was covered with real, growing grass to commemorate the installment of the Cardinals' new natural-grass field.

Ride the Redbird Express

WHERE: Near the Water Tower at 134 St. Clair Square in Fairview Heights, IL 62208

WHEN: First bus leaves two-and-a-half hours prior to Cardinals home games, with service every 10 minutes or so. See www.scctd .org/Special_redbird%20express.html for more details.

WHAT TO DO: Park your car and just hop on the bus, Gus

COST: $5 round trip for adults, $2 for children under 13.

BUCKET RANK: 🪣🪣

No doubt some reading this think the Redbird Express has something to do with calling on hard-throwing Cardinals closer Trevor Rosenthal to finish a game. We're not talking about riding *that* Redbird Express. We're talking buses here.

Back in the early 1950s, as people continued to flock to the suburbs, St. Louis' antiquated streetcar system became less practical and less popular. The metropolitan bus system began operating the "Redbird Express," a line specifically dedicated to efficiently transporting people to the old ballpark—aka Sportsman's Park, later renamed Busch Stadium.

Servicing strategic arteries around the metropolitan area, making limited stops on the way, the buses whisked eager baseball fans down to bustling Grand Avenue. In the early 1960s, there were more than 1,200 buses operating in St. Louis. Today, there are 400.

But all these years later, the Redbird Express is still in operation, operated by the St. Clair (Illinois) Transit District. A shadow of its former self, with only one route and one pickup point, the old R&E is still a terrific and economical way to and from a Cardinals game.

You can even combine a little shopping or dining with the trip to the ballpark. The Redbird Express runs out of St. Clair Square in Fairview Heights, Illinois, where there are some 130 shops and restaurants for you to enjoy. You could stop in St. Louis Dugout and pick up something Cardinals oriented to wear, or, if you're taking small children, you can get to the mall early to allow them time at the new indoor play area. It features more than 1,000 square feet of soft, colorful structures for climbing and exploring.

Maybe the little whippersnappers will work some of the energy out and actually sit still at the baseball game—for half an inning or so.

Park the car at the mall and the Redbird Express bus will take you straight to Busch Stadium. You can catch one two-and-a-half hours before the game or as late as 30 minutes before. The ride is some

10–15 minutes long. Unlike the Metro trains, there are no stops and no crowds with which to deal.

If you want to ride the Metro, there is a train station conveniently located right next to the ballpark. If you're willing to walk some distance, you might find $5 parking several blocks north of the ballpark. Otherwise, you'd have a hard time beating hassle-free bus transportation to and from the stadium for $5 and $2.

You are encouraged, if you are coming with a group of 25 or more, to let the Redbird Expressians (St. Clair County Transit District) know ahead of time. Email them at info@scctd.org; a response usually takes 30 minutes or so.

Then, as the old Greyhound bus commercials used to say, "Sit back, relax, and leave the driving to us." Just make sure you have the exact cash fare, please.

All Redbird Express buses are wheelchair lift equipped and unload/load outside Gate 4 at Busch Stadium, which is the left field side of the ballpark, at the corner of 7th and Clark.

After the game, Redbird Express buses will be lined up at the same corner. As you leave the old yard, board the front bus. Once that vehicle has a seated load, it will be the first to push off and return you to your regular programming at St. Clair Square.

Don't worry; if there is a rain delay or extra innings and you want to beat a retreat, the buses will be waiting outside. Once there are enough passengers to warrant a return trip, that bus will head back. Always go to the front bus unless instructed otherwise.

Under normal circumstances, the last bus leaves the ballpark for the return trip 25 minutes after the official end of the game.

Despite the fact that it is located in Illinois and is the only such service, the Redbird Express boarded more than 200,000 passengers during the 2014 season. Makes you wonder if it wouldn't make sense to resuscitate the service points in the St. Louis metro area.

Then again, that bus has already left the barn, so to speak.

There are numerous dates on the Cardinals' calendar that include postgame activities, such as Christian Day or "Run the Bases." The Redbird Express may not be able to accommodate those who want to stay for such events. The last bus leaves the stadium 45 minutes after the game, so you may need to leave the activities early in order to catch the last bus.

As for normal bus activities, such as sticking "ABC" (already been chewed) gum under a seat, playing musical chairs, or chanting "99 Bottles of Beer" or "Take Me Out to the Ball Game," those are entirely at the patron's discretion.

Cross the Stan Musial Bridge and Visit Donora, Pennsylvania

WHERE: Across the Monongahela River between Donora and Monessen, Pennsylvania

WHEN: Like Jerry Rice, always open

WHAT TO DO: Find the town of Donora on a map of western Pennsylvania and cross the bridge to get there

COST: Travel expenses to get there will vary, depending on where you're coming from

BUCKET RANK: 🪣🪣🪣🪣🪣

Donora is a borough in Washington County, Pennsylvania, some 20 miles south of Pittsburgh, on a sharp bend in the Monongahela River. The Stan Musial Bridge, so named in 2012, carries traffic across the Monongahela River between Donora and Monessen. If you're traveling on I-70, you will wind up taking the bridge into town.

If you're a Cardinals fan, you know Donora as sacred ground, the birthplace and childhood home of the greatest Cardinal ever—Stan Musial. Long before he became known as "the Man," Stanislaw Franciszek Musial was known as "Donora Greyhound" in this small corner of western Pennsylvania.

Donora is a "Rust Belt" town, once anchored by U.S. Steel's American Steel & Wire plant, which churned out wire, nails, and fences; and the Donora Zinc Works, where products were galvanized to become rust resistant.

The city promotes itself as the "Home of Champions" because of the number of famous athletes it has produced, including Musial, former NFL running back "Deacon" Dan Towler, and former Cincinnati Reds standout Ken Griffey Sr. Musial played baseball with Griffey's father, Buddy Griffey.

But outside of sports, the city is best known for the "Donora Smog of 1948," an air inversion that trapped industrial effluent from the factories over the city for five days. Twenty people died during that period, and another 50 died after the air pollution dispersed. Among those who lost their lives in the latter group was Lukasz Musial, Stan's father.

But Musial escaped the mills through baseball. He began playing when he was eight years old. A feature about Musial in a Donora newspaper once noted, "While still a kid in knee pants, Stan was very seldom at home and nearly always could be found wearing a dilapidated baseball glove while cavorting about a diamond."

Musial was introduced to the game by a neighbor, Joe Barbao, who was a former minor league pitcher. At the age of 14, Musial was among a group of kids that formed a Donora junior city league team called the Heslep All-Stars.

In their first game, the All-Stars beat a team from the more affluent side of the tracks, Cement City, 24–2. Musial pitched and batted fifth, going 4-for-5 and striking out 14 batters. By the summer of 1936, he was the batboy for the Donora Zincs, an industrial-league team managed by Barbao.

On one steamy August night, with his pitching staff spent, Barbao asked his batboy if he'd like to try throwing an inning or two. In his book, *The Man Stan: Musial Then and Now*, written with Hall of Fame *St. Louis Post-Dispatch* sportswriter Bob Broeg, Musial remembered his excitement:

"Ever since a teacher forced me to write right-handed as a child, I've stammered when I was excited," he explained. "This time, I was speechless."

Lost for words, maybe. Lost with a baseball in his hand? Never. The 5'4", 140-pound Musial, then a boy playing among men, pitched six innings and struck out 13.

Another of those who helped Musial along the way was Michael "Ki" Duda, a teacher and athletic coach at Donora High School. The school went 15 years without fielding a baseball team. But in the spring of 1938, with 17-year-old Stan Musial available, Duda revived the program.

In his only high school season, Musial pitched, played outfield, and batted cleanup for the Dragon Diamondeers. The school publication noted on April 13, 1938, Musial allowed three hits and retired 17 of 21 batters on strikeouts to lead Donora to a 3–2 victory over neighboring Monessen. The deciding run was scored when Musial singled home teammate Buddy Griffey.

As a pitcher, Duda once observed, Musial possessed a blazing fastball. "The problem with him as a schoolboy pitcher," Duda explained, "was we couldn't find anyone who could catch him. He might strike out 18 men, but half of them would get to first on dropped third strikes."

The 9–3 Dragon Diamondeers were the Mon Valley High School champions that spring. Musial finished 4–2 as a pitcher. He struck out 14 in one of the losses, but his team committed three fielding errors behind him. In his other defeat, Musial allowed two hits.

At the plate, he batted .455 and was named to the All-Section team. In his final high school game, Musial pitched a two-hitter and struck out 12 to lead Donora past Monongahela. He also went 3-for-3, with a single, triple, and home run. Naturally, the home run came in his last at-bat, a shot over the center fielder's head.

Cardinals scout Andrew French eventually signed Musial as a pitcher and the southpaw spent his early days in the organization in that capacity. He was 18–5 for Class D Daytona Beach in 1940. But after he hurt his left arm tumbling for a ball in the outfield in the spring of 1941, Musial found a true calling as one of the iconic hitters in the game.

To those who saw him swing a bat in Donora, that came as no surprise. He once hit a home run at Legion Field in nearby Monongahela City that people talked about for years. As the story goes, his younger brother, Ed Musial, walked ahead of "Stash" to load the bases. Musial stepped in, turned on a fastball and sent it soaring over the right fielder's head.

The ball crashed against a fence 450 feet away before the right fielder retrieved it. By that time, both Musials had crossed the plate.

Sadly, that romantic tale aside, there is little left to see of Musial's boyhood home. The population pushed 14,000 when the Musial family lived in the "Polish Hill" section of town. At one time, the factories lining the riverfront employed more than 5,000. But that industrial boom evaporated and the population of the entire town now hovers at 5,000.

The house on the hill where Musial grew up on the north side is gone. The grade school he went to is long gone, replaced by townhouses. The junior high school he attended is a vacant lot. The Legion Field behind where the high school stood is still there, overrun with weeds and shrubs. Grandstands built into the hillside have been neglected; sections of chain-link fence surrounding the field are in disrepair.

The 2009 closing and 2015 demolition of the Donora-Webster Bridge, which carried Route 837 over the Monongahela River into downtown Donora, has contributed to the demise of the town. A four-lane bridge built in the 1970s crosses the river at the southern edge of town and allows traffic to bypass downtown Donora altogether.

During the late 1930s and early 1940s, McKean Avenue was alive with restaurants, jewelers, butcher shops, and tailors. There were six Catholic churches and a synagogue in town, as well as a brewery, a dairy, and a soda-processing plant.

Today, the church buildings are for sale. There are no schools and no grocery stores. The last three banks in town closed soon after the aforementioned bridge.

While he moved to St. Louis, Musial stayed connected to his hometown. He kept memberships in Donora clubs. He regularly sent a local physician boxes of autographed baseballs, which could be used to raise money for charities. In addition to the Stan Musial Bridge, the city named a ballfield in the park on the north end of town in Musial's honor.

Musial passed away in January 2013 at the age of 92. His hometown is still standing, but barely.

By the way, there also is a Stan Musial Veterans Memorial Bridge in St. Louis. The "Stan Span" is a bridge that crosses the Mississippi River connecting downtown St. Louis with St. Clair County, Illinois. It was built between April 19, 2010, and July 2013, then opened on February 9, 2014.

That works out well. Musial had an equal number of hits in his career (1,815) home and away. He also has an equal number of bridges (one) home and away.

. . . .

Cruise with the Cardinals

WHERE: Somewhere in the Caribbean

WHEN: In late January

WHAT TO DO: Go to the Altair Travel website (www.altairtravel. com) and sign up for the official St. Louis Cardinals Cruise. Or call Pat Blassie at 314-968-9600 or 1-800-264-1116 for details.

COST: The cruise ship may change from year to year, as do the prices. But generally, it will run from $1,200 to $1,700 depending on the cabin class. That price is per person based on double occupancy—cruise only. A third and fourth person in the cabin might be some $650–$700 per person. Fuel charges, port charges and government taxes were included in these rates and were subject to change by the cruise line. Airfare and round-trip airport/ pier transfers were additional.

BUCKET RANK: 🪣🪣🪣🪣

. . . .

Cruising is a popular form of vacationing. In 2015, statistics showed the cruise industry was realizing revenues of $37.85 billion annually. Cruises provide 314,000 jobs and accommodate 20,335,000 passengers, including 1,600,000 children.

Statistics also showed that, among the most appealing cruise destinations, the Caribbean ranks first with a 43 percent approval rate. So if you've always wanted to take a cruise, and you're a fan of Cardinals baseball, what could be better than cruising to Caribbean ports with some of your favorite ballplayers?

The Cardinals have been hosting a cruise nearly every year since 1986. That was the year Todd Worrell captured the National League Rookie of the Year Award, and Worrell has been among those to participate. As with fantasy camps, fan fests, and other activities, it is a way to satisfy the insatiable appetite of some to have a closer, more personal experience with the players and the organization.

The Cardinals Cruise has attracted as many as 250 people in some years. From the time you show up at the port of departure, joining dozens of others in Cardinals jerseys and caps, to the time you relax on deck, sunning next to one of your favorites, you feel like a member of the team.

A personalized identification badge is provided to each Cardinals Cruise passenger, which serves as a "ticket" to attend all of the private events, including cocktail parties, a question-and-answer session, a photo session, and an autograph session with the cruising Cardinals celebrities.

For 2016, the trip includes a seven-day cruise to the eastern Caribbean on the good ship Celebrity Reflection, January 23–30. The ship leaves from Miami on Saturday, and cruises to San Juan, Puerto Rico; Phillipsburg, St. Maarten; and Charlotte Amalie, St. Thomas, before returning to Miami on the following Saturday.

The U.S. News & World Report Travel website (www.travel.usnews .com/cruises) has good things to say about the ship, including this: "Launched in October 2012, the 3,046-passenger Celebrity Reflection is Celebrity's newest ship. With more features than its Solstice-class siblings, including a top-deck Lawn Club complete with an art studio and open-air grill, along with three additional suite class categories, the Celebrity Reflection sets itself apart from its mainstream competitors."

The Cardinals Cruise lineup of celebrities changes from year to year, with different members of management, current players, and past players on board. The one constant is Fredbird, who makes every trip and keeps both kids and adults entertained. And not every experience is structured or planned. In 2008, a Cardinals Cruise member was trying to climb aboard a banana boat in the Dominican Republic when the boat tipped over. It tossed the petrified passenger into the water, trapping her underneath.

Joe Mather, a Cardinals utility player at the time, jumped in the water and rescued the passenger—Carolyn Chamberlain of East Peoria, Illinois. "He saved my life," Chamberlain told MLB.com. So you see, Mather not only was useful late in a game, when you needed a pinch-hitter or a double switch. He could also come to the forefront in save situations.

Good to know, should you in any way be unsettled by the fact that since 1979, 55 cruise ships have sunk.

There is practical reason for all this fun in the sun. Proceeds go to benefit the club's charitable arm, Cardinals Care. Redbird Rookies, the flagship program of Cardinals Care, aspires to give thousands of kids an opportunity to play baseball and learn life lessons in the process. That mission is achieved through a variety of programs, which allow for cash grants to support organizations in and around St. Louis.

On the final night of a Cardinals Cruise, the group will gather for dinner and uphold a tradition that captures both the prevailing spirit of the cruise and optimism for the fast-approaching new season. Pat Blassie and John Berra, owners of St. Louis–based Altair Travel, will rise from their table and lead the group in a heartfelt rendition of "Take Me Out to the Ball Game."

For those of us who might never get the opportunity to sing it from the broadcast booth at Wrigley Field, it's not a bad alternative.

BE CAREFUL NOT TO CRUISE TOO EARLY

As mentioned, a Cardinals Cruise has become a popular way for St. Louis baseball fans to vacation. However, the team has to be careful about when it cruises. For instance, the Cardinals cruise began a little too early late in the 1964 season.

Having made up six games in 12 days, the soaring Redbirds had a one-half-game lead in the National League when they opened the final series of the '64 season at home against the New York Mets. The Cardinals were riding an eight-game winning streak at the time.

The last-place Mets, carrying 108 losses already, had lost eight in a row and 17 of the last 20. They were 41 games out of first place.

In the meantime, the two other teams still in the hunt for the NL pennant—Philadelphia and Cincinnati—were battling head to head in the Queen City, knocking each other off. In other words, with three games to play, the Cardinals' come-from-behind pennant chase appeared to be consummated.

In short, the Cardinals could start the cruise...or so it seemed.

With 18-game winner Bob Gibson pitching the opening game of the series on Friday, October 2, the Cardinals were poised to clinch at least a tie for the National League crown. And sure enough, big-game Gibson was as advertised, allowing the Mets just one run and striking out seven in eight innings. Cardinals closer Barney Schultz then added a shutout ninth inning to back Gibson's performance.

Problem was, diminutive left-hander Al Jackson was even better. The Mets' ace, who later would win 13 games for the Cardinals in 1966, somehow won 11 in 1964 for this horrible Mets team. With more than 19,000 on hand at Busch Stadium (old Sportsman's Park), Jackson limited the Cardinals to five hits and snapped their winning streak with a 1–0 shutout win.

Not to worry. The club had 20-game winner Ray Sadecki ready to pitch the second game of the series. As the day started, they were still in first place, still enjoying a half-game lead over the Reds. But the cruise officially ended three hours, 14 minutes later.

Sadecki was a disaster, giving up four runs in the first and leaving after getting only three outs. His performance put Cardinals manager Johnny Keane in a predicament where he had to use seven more pitchers and ravage his bullpen. The Mets smashed 17 hits and five home runs on their way to a 15–5 win.

The Cardinals fell into a tie with the Reds atop the standings. All of a sudden, the pennant was up for grabs with one game to play. All of a sudden, the lowly Metropolitans were the Cardinals' worst nightmare.

With more than 30,146 in the stands for the season finale on October 4, the Cardinals sent lefty Curt Simmons to the mound and hoped for the best. An 18-game winner, Simmons was not at his best. He went less than five innings deep into the game, allowing seven hits and three runs. When they came to bat in the bottom of the fifth, the Cardinals trailed 3–2.

But the Cardinals rallied for three in the fifth, with Ken Boyer, Dick Groat, and light-hitting Dal Maxvill knocking in runs. With the bullpen depleted, Keane turned to Gibson, who had pitched just two nights earlier. In a heroic performance, Gibson threw four more innings. He wasn't at his sharpest, walking five and allowing two runs.

But he bought the Cardinals time, as they erupted for three more runs in the sixth and three in the eighth, with Bill White and Curt Flood hitting home runs. This time, Schultz finished it off for his 14th save, Gibson was credited with his 19th win and, finally, the Cardinals were able to beat the Mets 11–5.

With the scoreboard posting Philadelphia's 10–0 victory at Cincinnati, the Cardinals clinched and the Busch Stadium crowd celebrated the team's first pennant in 18 years. They would go on to stun the New York Yankees in a memorable seven-game series and capture a world championship.

And the lesson? Cruising is best done after the season.

Get Opening Day in St. Louis Declared a Civic Holiday

Opening Day in the Major Leagues is special around the country. Opening Day in St. Louis is a religious experience, a day in the city unlike any other. The television stations, radio stations, and print media are all over it from morning to evening. Bands play, rallies rage downtown, festivities surround the ballpark, tributes and ceremonies go on inside the ballpark. There's even a baseball game conducted at some point.

Between the ceremonial pitches, the motorcade introduction of Cardinals Hall of Fame Players and the current rosters, the Budweiser Clydesdale, the bald eagle from the Wild Bird Sanctuary, and the presentation of colors, it is a wondrous marriage between a historic past and a hopeful future. There is something for everyone,

It is almost a civic duty, if you live in St. Louis, to put on some type of Cardinals gear, join the "sea of red," and embrace the sense of community and excitement that Opening Day fosters. For the record, the Cardinals are 71–62–1 in Opening Days in St. Louis. Off the record, there's no such thing as an unsuccessful Opening Day.

In 2015, Jan and Dan Daniels attended their 58th consecutive Cardinals opener in St. Louis. They saw their first one in 1957 at Sportsman's Park. Stan Musial went hitless and the Cardinals lost to the Chicago Cubs 10–2 that day. Not even that was enough to discourage the Danielses.

Moreover, as they sat through a 5–4 loss to the Brewers on the April 13th opener in St. Louis in 2015, there was one thing in particular

Opening Day is like a holiday for Cardinals fans—but it isn't officially, at least not yet. Perhaps you could change that. (Jeff Curry-USA TODAY Sports)

the couple missed about that first Opening Day at the old ballpark on Grand Ave.

"We were younger then," said Dan Daniels, 82 at the time.

For players who have never experienced the love, a St. Louis opener can be disarming. Outfielder Jason Heyward had been through several fine openers in Atlanta. But when he was in the lineup for the Cardinals' opener against Milwaukee in 2015, it had a different feel.

"You see tailgating, you see people camping out, you sense tradition here," Heyward said. "It's really something special."

Heyward was so taken aback by the rousing reception he got, he jumped out of the pickup truck that carried him around the stadium to home plate and didn't know where to go. He jogged right past the lineup of Cardinals luminaries waiting to shake his hand,

CALL IN SICK

Getting Opening Day proclaimed a holiday will take considerable effort and may take some time. It's entirely possible hell could freeze over in the interim.

That being the case, Cardinals fans who hold down a steady job or go to school will have to be bold and creative when it comes to taking the day off. It's tricky business.

For one, the United States is the only one of the wealthiest nations in the world that does not guarantee workers the right to paid sick leave. Since 2006, when San Francisco blazed the trail, cities and states have been adopting their own sick-leave legislation. But as of 2015, only four states and 19 cities in the country had laws guaranteeing sick leave.

It's enough to make you sick.

CareerBuilder, a global human resources and recruiting company, conducted a survey that indicated workers are rolling the dice when they offer up lame excuses. According to the numbers, nearly one in five employers (18 percent) said they had fired an employee for calling in sick with a fake excuse. One in four of the employers (24 percent) said they caught an employee lying about being sick by checking social media.

Food for thought here: if you call the office and tell them you're too sick to come in, don't take selfies at the ballpark with Fredbird and post them on Facebook.

Just sayin'….

And on the subject of common sense, keep one other thing in mind. Chances are, your employer is not an idiot—a reality that seems to escape many employees. Under the category of "truth can be stranger than fiction," employers who responded to the Harris Poll reported these top 10 worst excuses for missing work:

- Employee just put a casserole in the oven.

- Employee's plastic surgery for enhancement purposes needed some "tweaking" to get it just right.

- Employee was sitting in the bathroom and her feet and legs fell asleep. When she stood, up she fell and broke her ankle.

- Employee had been at the casino all weekend and still had money left to play with on Monday morning.

- Employee woke up in a good mood and didn't want to ruin it.

- Employee had a "lucky night" and didn't know where he was.

- Employee got stuck in the blood pressure machine at the grocery store and couldn't get out.

- Employee had a gallstone they wanted to heal holistically.

- Employee caught their uniform on fire by putting it in the microwave to dry.

- Employee accidentally got on a plane.

There is a bottom line here. That is, it's Opening Day and it is your God-given right as a Cardinals fan to wear red, cheer Clydesdales, and celebrate baseball, be it in person, on television, or streaming live. Until Opening Day is declared a holiday, until your city or state adopts a paid sick-leave law, calling in sick will be the risk of doing business.

With that in mind, here are some more tried and true, reasonable excuses to consider:

Contagious illness, such as the common cold or flu.
With employers more fearful about starting an epidemic in the office, there's no more reliable reason to miss work than a legitimate sickness, especially if it involves a fever or coughing. Two keys: make sure you sound like you are in intensive care when you call the office and make sure you are not seen by anyone who might blow the whistle.

Doctor's appointment
Another old standby. Problem is, this excuse has holes. Some employers might simply give you the day, others will expect you to miss only half the day. This requires time-management skills. Be smart about when your "scheduled appointment" takes place.

Car broke down
Like the others, totally believable. But, like the appointment excuse, could be time restricted. However, if the repair is substantial enough—"They're saying they're going to have to replace the transmission"—you should have no problem milking it for a whole day. Again, be heard, not seen.

I've earned it
Hey, performance carries a lot of weight. Go in early, stay late for a week or two, and make sure the right people notice. You should have no problem negotiating a day off.

Andrea Nierenberg, president of The Nierenberg Group, a management consulting and personal marketing practice, put it this way: "Really work when you're there, so you'll be able to feel good about taking time off."

Or suck up, whatever works. Chances are you'll feel good either way.

Need a personal day for a family issue

This could be about a sick child, injured dog, ailing mother, or some other family emergency. However, stay away from a death in the family. That is a particularly intolerable lie and if it's discovered, questions about your moral character will haunt you the rest of your life.

Someone just gave me box seats to the game

Sometimes embellishing a truth can be effective. A lot of employers would be sympathetic to the fact that such an opportunity just dropped in your lap. If it works, you can even take the selfie with Fredbird.

Entertaining clients

This doesn't work for everyone. It's sort of based on an idea that you have clients and there would be a reason for you to entertain them on company time.

I'm having cramps

Effective, but once again, not for everyone.

Toilet exploded

Just about everyone has been there and can relate to this kind of predicament. What's more, companies can never give a specific time when repairmen might arrive, which can result in one sitting around all day waiting. Hence, the day off.

Working from home

In today's laptop world, this has become a real option. Problem is, you likely will have to get some actual work done, either before or after baseball activities. So either get a very early start, or go easy on ice-cold, frosty ones.

momentarily snubbing the likes of Bob Gibson, Red Schoendienst, and Lou Brock. Manager Mike Matheny caught Heyward and sent him back for the proper protocol.

Matheny played five seasons in St. Louis, but he also played in San Francisco, Toronto, and Milwaukee. The experience at Busch Stadium is one of a kind.

"Everybody has their own traditions for Opening Day," Matheny said. "It just seems like it's a little bigger here, a little deeper as far as things that have been going on for a long time....How many people get to ride around in front of 40,000 people and have them cheer?"

For bucket-list pursuers, there is good news. This correspondent has already written and recorded an Opening Day theme song to spur the civic holiday movement. Have a listen at http://www .liberateyourbrand.com/blog/holiday-music-for-opening-day.

A creative promotions company in St. Louis, the Switch, got the ball rolling with a "Make It a Holiday" initiative in 2014. Part of the mission statement read as follows:

"Opening Day: Make It a Holiday" is an initiative that has been gaining momentum since 2008. This year, celebrating St. Louis' 250th anniversary, the target is to set a world record for opening day by getting 250,000 people to participate. Use the hashtag #openingdayholiday to participate and help Make Opening Day a Holiday."

So you see, a blueprint has already been established. All the bucket-list crowd has to do is play it forward.

Get Over 1985

No season has had more bittersweet elements to it than the Cardinals' pennant-winner of 1985. It was a remarkable season in many ways. The club won 101 games, the most by a Cardinals team in 18 years and the most for another 19 seasons, or until the 2004 team won 105.

With mercurial Vince Coleman leading the way with 110 steals, the '85 club had 314 stolen bases. The American League Oakland Athletics had 341 steals in 1976. But the '85 collection of bags was the most by a St. Louis edition since the American Association teams of the 1880s and remains the most by any National League team over the past 113 years. The New York Giants had 319 steals in 1912.

In addition to Coleman winning the NL Rookie of the Year Award, Willie McGee captured a batting title with a .353 average and was named the league's Most Valuable Player. The Cardinals had five names among the top 11 in the MVP voting.

Second baseman Tom Herr had an amazing season in which he collected 110 RBIs while hitting only eight home runs. He is still the last NL player to drive in 100 or more runs in a season while hitting fewer than 10 home runs. He batted .356 with men on base that season, and an astounding .556 with runners at second and third. If ever a stat cries out "intentional walk," that's it.

Then there was the pitching, which featured three starters that combined for 60 wins—Joaquin Andujar (21), John Tudor (21), and Danny Cox (18). The club had not had a more dominating starting trio since the 1935 team had four starters combine for 75 wins, led by Dizzy Dean's 28 wins and Paul Dean's 19. Andujar and Tudor were the first two Cardinals starters to get 20 or more wins in the same season since Mort Cooper (22) and Johnny Beasley (21) in 1942.

Everything the Cardinals did seemingly came up roses. Late in the season, they added veteran outfielder Cesar Cedeno for depth. Cedeno went berserk, batting .434 with six homers and 19 RBIs in 76 at-bats. They brought up Todd Worrell to help the bullpen and Worrell went 3–0 with five saves in 17 appearances.

Manager Whitey Herzog won a world championship with the 1982 Cardinals, and won another pennant with his 1987 club. But there's no question in his mind which was the best team he managed.

"With the way we could play defense, run the bases, and the starting pitching, I'd have to say it was the '85 club, Herzog said. "I mean, when we went into a series with Tudor, Andujar, and Coxie, we had a pretty good idea we were going to win at least two out of three."

Then came the postseason and weird things started happening. First a stadium tarp tried to swallow Coleman. The incident took place on the field before Game 4 of the National League Championship Series.

As the Cardinals' workout ended, Coleman lingered on the field and had his back turned to the stands when the Busch Stadium automated tarpaulin was activated. While opposing catchers were having a heckuva time trying to catch "Vincent Van Go," the "killer tarp," which weighed more than a half ton and was 180 feet in length, ran the unaware Coleman down and momentarily pinned his leg.

X-rays revealed a small bone fracture in Coleman's left knee, and he was done for the remainder of the postseason.

"To this day," Herzog said in 2015, "I still don't know how the fastest guy in the major leagues gets caught by a tarp moving about 2 miles an hour. I've never really had that explained to me."

Initially, there was an improbable counterdevelopment to the incident. The Cardinals hit only 87 home runs all season, the fewest in the majors. But without Coleman sparking their speed game, they found their slugging shoes.

Ozzie Smith and Jack Clark hit dramatic home runs to win Games 5 and 6, and the Cardinals beat the Los Angeles Dodgers to advance to the World Series, or the "I-70 Series," with the Kansas City Royals.

Then, something ominous happened again.

Leading the World Series three games to two, leading 1–0 in Game 6, three outs from a championship, with Worrell on the mound in the ninth inning, adversity struck. Jorge Orta led off the ninth for Kansas City with a tap to first. Jack Clark fielded and tossed to Worrell, who reached out to touch the base ahead of Orta. Umpire Don Denkinger called Orta safe.

Instead of one out and none on, there were no outs with the tying run on base in the speedy Orta. The Cardinals self-destructed, losing the game 2–1, then losing a 11–0 humiliation in Game 7.

For more than 30 years since, Cardinals fans have blamed Denkinger's call, the tarp—anyone and anything for the 1985 championship that got away.

But shake your arms, bend your neck side to side a few times, take a deep breath, and accept the reality. The Cardinals—not Denkinger, not the tarp, not an evil spirit—were the culpable party. After Orta reached, Jack Clark muffed a foul pop and catcher Darrell Porter had a passed ball, allowing runners to move to second and third. And Porter was inexplicably in poor position to receive right fielder Andy Van Slyke's perfect throw that should have nailed Kansas City's Jim Sundberg and prevented the winning run from scoring.

What's more, Game 6 didn't win the World Series; it only tied it. The Cardinals still had a chance to win the Series in Game 7 with 21-game winner Andujar on the mound.

The truth is, the Cardinals didn't win the 1985 World Series because they stole just two bases in five attempts over seven games. They didn't win because Clark went homerless, Herr batted .154, Cedeno batted .133, Ozzie Smith batted .087, and Van Slyke batted .091.

Those 101 wins, those 314 steals, that "Whiteyball" excitement: all contingent on the Cardinals actually getting on base once in a while. But against the Royals, the Cardinals managed just 40 hits in 216 at-bats, the fewest hits ever collected in a seven-game series. Their .185 batting average was the worst team average in World Series history for a seven-game series. They scored 13 runs in seven games, including two over the final 31 innings.

"In fairness," Herzog said, "the Kansas City starting staff shut us down. We could have won getting only 13 runs in six games. As it was, we got 13 runs in seven games.

"We had to play baseball like everybody else, which we couldn't do. Our base stealers never got on base....We never had the opportunity to play our game in the World Series."

You have no right to blame an umpire when you make mistakes and give the other team extra outs. You're not supposed to win a World Series when your offense completely shuts down.

In other words, get over it.

It was a season to cherish, a World Series to regret. Nothing less, and nothing more.

Forgive Don Denkinger

Baseball adopted instant replay in 2014 and has been refining it ever since. If the technology had been in use during the 1985 World Series, the ninth inning of Game 6 might have gone differently. The Cardinals might have 12 world championships instead of 11.

But the operative phrase there is "might have," not would have.

To hold Don Denkinger responsible for what took place instead is just infantile. There is still a human element involved. Umpires miss calls; it happens all the time. Before replay came along, those misses largely went uncorrected.

The use of instant replay has done nothing if not underlined how difficult it is, how quickly things happen, how many different angles it takes to see things correctly. Even the results of replay are sometimes inconclusive. In real time, umpires have one angle, one speed, and one shot to get it right. Remarkably, they do most of the time.

Denkinger was a terrific umpire, among the best in the American League from 1969 to 1998. The fact he was working that World Series and worked three others (1974, 1980, and 1991) was testament to his skills. He also worked three All-Star Games and several other postseason series.

He was the home-plate umpire for the one-game playoff that decided the AL's Eastern Division champion in 1978, when the New York Yankees defeated the Boston Red Sox on Bucky Dent's home run. Only the umpires who grade out the best work in those events.

Denkinger is also a human being, one who has been married to the same woman for more than 50 years, one who turns 80 years of age in 2016. Yes, slow-motion replay indicated he missed the call in that ninth inning of Game 6 in 1985.

He called leadoff batter Jorge Orta safe when Orta should have been out. The controversial call was part of an inning that saw the Royals rally from a 1–0 deficit, win 2–1, and capture the Series in seven games. Before they could be challenged and overturned, such mistakes were part of the game, sometimes at the worst moments.

It wasn't the first time, and it wasn't the last. In 2010, Armando Galarraga's perfect game was ruined by a blown call at first base by umpire Jim Joyce.

Those who have used Denkinger's mistake as a crutch all these years, including members of the 1985 club, are in denial. Those who blame Denkinger for everything that took place in that fateful inning are looking for an emotional way out. Those who assume the Cardinals would have won had the call gone differently assume a lot.

As Colonel Jessep from *A Few Good Men* might say, they "can't handle the truth."

In 2014 when the Royals made it back to the World Series, the Denkinger play was revisited in stories and interviews. Jamie Quirk, a catcher on the '85 Royals team, put it in perspective:

"Look, he was out," Quirk said. "But when the play happened, watching it with the naked eye, you kind of thought Todd Worrell was off the bag. We're sitting there in the dugout, yelling, 'Safe!' It wasn't as obvious as everyone thinks.

"And other things happened, too. How about Jack Clark missing that pop-up? Couldn't the Cardinals have gotten out of that inning with a runner on and nobody out? Does a bad call mean you have to lose 11–0 in the next game?"

The Cardinals—not Denkinger—self-destructed. The next Royals hitter, Steve Balboni, popped up on the first pitch. The foul ball drifted over by the Royals' dugout. Cardinals first baseman Jack Clark got under the ball, then inexplicably hesitated as catcher Darrell Porter came into view. Clark tried to pick up the ball again and missed it. What should have been an automatic out fell untouched. A reprieved Balboni followed with a single and Orta moved to second.

Onix Concepcion pinch ran for Balboni at first. Royals catcher Jim Sundberg attempted to advance the runners with a sacrifice bunt, but Worrell fielded it and retired the lead runner at third. That good play was followed by another critical Cardinals mistake.

With pinch-hitter Hal McRae at the plate, Porter was crossed up by a Worrell slider and missed connections. The passed ball accomplished

DON DENKINGER

It's sad to think what Denkinger went through during the years immediately following the 1985 World Series. St. Louis likes to think of itself as the best baseball city in America, but obviously it has its warts.

Denkinger received vicious hate mail for several years from Cardinals fans. Two St. Louis radio personalities helped fuel the fire by revealing a phone number and home address for Denkinger on the air.

"People were calling and saying they were going to burn the house down," Denkinger recalled.

In 1987, the FBI even had to be enlisted to investigate a letter (with no return address) that threatened to "blow away" Denkinger with a .357 Magnum. But like the call, Denkinger doesn't dwell on what took place in the aftermath.

"It's life and it goes on," said Denkinger, who now lives in Arizona. "I'm obviously reminded constantly that I made a mistake. You know what? I was an umpire for more than 30 years in the Major Leagues. I know I made a lot of mistakes. That one was just blown out of proportion."

Denkinger is often asked to autograph photos depicting the 1985 call, and he is happy to do so. He even owns a painting featuring himself, Todd Worrell, and Jorge Orta involved in the play. He said it reminds him that no one is perfect and everyone makes mistakes.

In 2010, he was invited to attend a baseball writers' dinner in St. Louis, honoring the 25th anniversary of the 1985 club. The person he sat next to on the celebrity dais? Todd Worrell.

"If anyone could take it back, he would take it back," Worrell said. "He would love to change history and have it go away."

what Sundberg's bunt had not—putting runners at second and third with one out.

Worrell, a hard-throwing right-hander, then walked the right-handed-hitting McRae to set up a force-out at every base. That brought left-handed-hitting Dane Iorg to the plate and he blooped a single into right field. Concepcion scored easily but charging right fielder Andy Van Slyke made a perfect throw to the plate, a throw that might have retired Sundberg and kept the score tied.

But Porter was inexplicably a step away from the plate instead of blocking it. He had to reach back with the tag after receiving Van Slyke's throw and Sundberg slid in safely to win the game for Kansas City. Repeat, to win the game, not the series.

The Cardinals still had John Tudor ready to start Game 7 the next day. Tudor had had an unforgettable regular season, starting 1–7 before winning 20 of his last 21 decisions. He had allowed the Royals one run over 15 innings in the Series, winning Games 1 and 4, the latter with a complete-game shutout.

But in Game 7, the Royals chased Tudor from the game with two runs in the second inning and three runs in the third inning. They pounded the Cardinals' bullpen for six more in the fifth and turned the score into an 11–0 romp. The Cardinals' offense was flatlining, managing two singles to that point.

The game turned into one of the most embarrassing in franchise history. With Denkinger working behind the plate, Cardinals 21-game winner and resident hothead Joaquin Andujar entered during the scattered fifth inning and immediately got into it with Denkinger. He was ejected. At the same time, Herzog took the opportunity to confront the embattled umpire and blame "the call" a day earlier for the whole mess.

"We wouldn't even be here if you hadn't missed the f——ing call last night!" Herzog reportedly said.

Denkinger responded, "Well, if you guys weren't hitting .120 in this World Series, we wouldn't be here." The Cardinals wound up hitting .185 and producing 13 runs, the worst seven-game offense in World Series history.

They showed no offense, they showed no poise, and they were humiliated 11–0 in Game 7 to lose the World Series. They did that— the Cardinals, not Don Denkinger.

- -

Catch a Souvenir Ball at a Cardinals Game

One of the beauties of owning a baseball glove, for kids or adults, is the chance to take it to a game. You might just use it to catch an actual major league baseball, hit by an actual major league player, during an actual major league game.

Patrons are still allowed to bring gloves to Busch Stadium and other ballparks, should they feel so inspired. And they are still welcome to keep a baseball that flies into the stands.

What's more, the chances of coming home with a ball have increased dramatically over the years. The newer baseball stadiums generally have shorter outfield distances and less foul territory. Hence, balls fly into the stands more regularly.

At the same time, MLB's philosophy about souvenir balls has changed. Players often toss balls into the stands after the third out of an inning, during batting practice sessions, or while just sitting in the bullpen or dugout.

Some of the best things in life are free, and that includes the best souvenir a Cardinals fan can get at a game: a foul ball. Bringing your own glove will make it easier to catch.

During the 1970s and 1980s, citing insurance concerns, MLB frowned on such behavior and fined players or umpires who randomly tossed baseballs into the stands. You were more likely to have a player hand you a live grenade than an official major league ball.

Now, the treasured spheres are handed out like cheese samples at a Sam's Club store. A Rawlings baseball costs MLB around $3, but the league has determined that its ability to win friends and influence customers far outweighs the costs or insurance risks.

These days, according to MLB, approximately 900,000 baseballs are used each season, some 200,000 of those in games. Each team goes through approximately 30,000.

Home teams are required to have 90 new baseballs on hand for each game and teams go through an average of eight to 10 dozen of them every night. That means any given ball has a shelf life of about five or six pitches. If the ball is struck, hits the ground, or simply doesn't feel right, it's removed from play. It might be kept for batting practice or authentication purposes, or simply tossed into the seats.

That's to say nothing of 14 to 15 dozen balls that are used during pregame drills and batting practice, many of which also wind up in the stands. Tim McClelland, who began umpiring in 1983, estimates that teams go through twice as many baseballs as they used to.

"Baseballs scuff a lot easier than they used to," McClelland says. "We used to go through maybe only five dozen and now it's doubled. Whether it's more balls in the dirt or that they scuff easily, pitchers don't want to throw a ball that's scuffed."

The Cardinals make it clear fans are welcome to keep any foul ball or home run ball hit into the Busch Stadium III stands. They will also award anyone catching a foul ball with an honorary contract, if he or she wants to fill out the necessary information.

On the flip side, the club states on its website, "At no time should a foul ball or home run ball be thrown back on the field. Any guest interfering with a ball in play is subject to ejection. The Cardinals are not able to accommodate requests for player autographs on home run or foul balls. Guests should stay alert at all times for bats and balls leaving the playing field."

Safe to say, a ball caught in flight as it enters the stands, during an actual game, is the most desirable souvenir ball. Should that ball be struck by a favored player, and/or be caught with the glove you have lugged to the game for that express purpose, even better. That said, a ball handed or tossed into the stands by a favored player could trump the aforementioned souvenir, depending on the circumstances. For instance, should the provided ball come with established eye contact or a conversational exchange, all bets are off.

The crazed method—that is, running over grandmothers, knocking down 10-year-olds, and disrupting an entire seating section to corral a loose ball—is frowned upon by civilized society. Is it still a souvenir, yes, but only in a most despicable sense.

The ultimate souvenir experience, of course, would be to catch a home run ball struck by a favorite player under memorable circumstances. To that end, you will be hard pressed ever to match the experience of Phil Ozersky.

Ozersky was a 26-year-old genetic researcher at Washington University in 1998, and in the right place at the right time when Mark McGwire's 70th homer came sailing over the wall at Busch Stadium II. McGwire's second home run of the game on September 27, 1998, established the major league single-season record.

Three summers later, that mark was exceeded by Barry Bonds' 73 home runs. Since then, both totals have become tainted by revelations of steroid use.

Ozersky was able to snare McGwire's ball after it bounced through the hands of two coworkers. A short while later, he auctioned off the ball for $3 million, a sum paid by comic book author Todd McFarlane.

One of the first things Ozersky did with his winnings was build a handicapped-accessible home in Florida for his father, who had suffered a stroke 12 years earlier and lost use of his left side. Ozersky also donated $250,000 of his take to the Cardinals Care program, kept his job, and kept his late-model car at the time.

But he did allow himself at least one perk. He purchased a pair of Cardinals season tickets on the first-base side, 20 rows from the owner's box.

That's prime souvenir country.

Get Beaked by Fredbird

WHERE: Busch Stadium, 700 Clark Avenue, St. Louis, MO 63102, or any one of a number of charitable events in which Fredbird participates

WHEN: Could happen anytime during a Cardinals game

WHAT TO DO: Secure a ticket for a Cardinals home game. You are almost certain to bump into him at U.S. Cellular Family Pavilion, where he makes frequent appearances. The area is geared toward kids and is tucked behind the right-field bleachers by Gate 6 at Busch Stadium. The incorrigible bird especially likes to beak those who least expect it. But calling his name or saying something silly is likely to wind up with your head in his mouth. Insults like "Hey Fredbird, your beak is so big, I bet you can smell what I'm thinking" will get you nowhere.

COST: Cardinals tickets can cost anywhere from $11.20 to $500. Go to the website, www.cardinals.mlb.com, or call the Cardinals' ticket office at 314-345-9000 for details. Admission to the Family Pavilion area is free.

BUCKET RANK:

A ccording to the Cardinals' website, the Cardinals mascot has "beaked" approximately "1,000,000,000,000,000,000,000,000,000,0 00" fans. Now, that may be a rather ambitious estimate. And frankly, if it's accurate, the St. Louis Health Department may have some concerns.

But seriously, ever since Fredbird hatched in 1979, he has been running around the field on an ATV or in his truck, dancing on dugouts, shooting T-shirts into the stands, and covering the heads of adoring fans—young and old—with his elongated, yellow beak.

Fredbird began his 38th season with the team in 2016 and is purported to have a "lifelong" contract. Among active Cardinals, only Hall of Fame Player Red Schoendienst has worn the Bird on the Bat longer.

In fact, Fredbird has his own team, made up of 11 cheerleading girls. Team Fredbird debuted in 1995 and has been helping the incorrigible bird create memories and madcap fun at the ballpark for millions of baseball fans.

What's more, Fredbird has his own television show. *Cardinals Kids* airs on Fox Sports Midwest three times a week from April through September, including 11:00 AM Saturdays, 2:00 PM Mondays, and 2:00 PM Wednesdays. The program features former Cardinals pitcher Andy Benes, local radio personality and stadium announcer "Professor" John Ulett, and, of course, the anthropomorphic cardinal wearing the team's home uniform.

Benes won 18 games for the Cardinals (18–10) and finished third in the Cy Young balloting in 1996. Over his 14-year career, which included stops in San Diego, Seattle, and Arizona, and two turns in St. Louis, he won 155 games and collected 2,000 strikeouts.

Benes is the older brother of Alan Benes, who also pitched for the Cardinals. Alan Benes won 22 of 57 appearances for the club during 1996–97 and seemed on his way to stardom. But an arm injury caused Alan to miss the entire 1998 season and he was never able to recapture his best form.

Andy Benes is not related to Fredbird, per se, but he is 6'6", which allows him to match up visually with the 6'3" Fredbird. What's more, Andy Benes and his wife, Jennifer, have five children, so he knows something about communicating with both mascots and kids.

Fredbird, the Cardinals' anthropomorphic mascot, is a fan favorite. His signature move is "beaking" young fans, or placing his entire mouth around their head. (Jasen Vinlove–USA Today Sports)

FREDBIRD

Fredbird, the official mascot of the Cardinals, was introduced in April 1979. He is an anthropomorphic cardinal wearing the team's uniform. Or, for those unwilling to accept the burlesque characterization, he is a person dressed as an anthropomorphic cardinal wearing the team's uniform.

As of 2015, the Cardinals were one of 27 MLB teams to have an official mascot. The Chicago Cubs were once managed by Don Zimmer, but they did not officially join the mascot community until introducing "Clark" the cub in 2014. Three teams—the Yankees, Dodgers, and Angels—still did not have official mascots, although one might argue Tommy Lasorda fits the bill unofficially for the Dodgers.

Interestingly enough, there were 35 mascots among the 27 teams. The Cincinnati Reds like mascots so much they had four of them, including Mr. Red, his female counterpart Rosie Red, Mr. Redlegs, and Gapper.

Like all of his kind, Fredbird specializes in entertaining young children during baseball games. His name is derived from "Redbird," a synonym for the cardinal bird and for the Cardinals themselves.

He is one of the more easily recognizable mascots in the game, popular with fans for his dancing, posing for photos, and shooting T-shirts into the stands. But he has built his reputation on "beaking" the heads of unsuspecting supporters.

Since 1995, he has been joined in his endeavors by a group of a dozen young women known as "Team Fredbird." They do not beak anyone.

Fredbird's look has changed a number of times over the years. Initially, he had feathers on his body, but overly enthusiastic fans were inclined to pluck one as a souvenir. He also had giant bird feet for the first few years of his existence, but mobility was an issue. Fredbird now wears big red sneakers.

He did have competition for attention when the Rally Squirrel became a secondary mascot for the Cardinals, born from an incident in the 2011 postseason. An actual squirrel appeared on the Busch Stadium field in the fifth inning of Game 4 of the National League Division Series, sprinting across home plate as Philadelphia pitcher Roy Oswalt delivered to Cardinals hitter Skip Schumaker. Oswalt complained that he was distracted by the squirrel and video of the incident became popular. Local businesses in St. Louis began creating products to capitalize on the incident.

An anthropomorphic squirrel wearing the team's uniform (No. 11) was introduced and a performer dressed as Rally Squirrel took part in fan rallies beginning with Game 3 of the 2011 National League Championship Series. The squirrel became Fredbird's companion during the remainder of the postseason, assisting in entertaining the Cardinals fans at Busch Stadium.

Rally Squirrel was even subtly depicted on the World Series rings the Cardinals received for winning the 2011 world championship. However, Rally Squirrel did not have the staying power of Fredbird and never became an official mascot.

The show teaches children about the game, the equipment, and the operations that take place at the stadium. Among the regular features is a phrase of the week, which explains terms of baseball vernacular, such as "five o'clock hitter," "flashing the leather," and "in the hole." As Fredbird believes strongly in being seen and not heard, Benes and Ulett handle most of the speaking responsibilities.

While Fredbird is an attraction at every Cardinals home game, he also gets out in the community, appearing at numerous Cardinals Care charity events and other philanthropic endeavors.

Fans can make arrangements to have Fredbird appear at an event by calling the Fredbird Hotline at 314-345-9441, or emailing Gail Ruhling at gruhling@cardinals.com. There are three categories where Fredbird appearances are concerned: 30 minutes for $150, 1 hour for $350, and 2 hours for $600. The rates may change if the appearance involves Fredbird traveling more than 50 miles from his nest at Busch Stadium.

Team Fredbird can also be booked for events, with or without their fearless leader. The women specialize in emceeing, selling raffle tickets, and pumping up enthusiasm. To book Team Fredbird, email teamfredbird@cardinals.com.

. . . .

Settle the Feud between Tony La Russa and Ozzie Smith

There have been great feuds throughout history—the Hatfields and McCoys, Al Capone and Bugs Moran, Jerry Lewis and Dean Martin, Alexander Hamilton and Aaron Burr. And there have been two great feuds in the history of the Cardinals.

The first was between Stan Musial and Joe Garagiola. The two were once best friends and business partners in St. Louis. But in the 1980s, they had a falling out over business matters concerning a bowling alley they co-owned, Red Bird Lanes. Garagiola filed a lawsuit and Musial never forgave him for it.

That became especially awkward before Game 5 of the 2006 World Series. A marketing person with the club was not aware of the bad feelings when he arranged to have Garagiola, Musial's teammate on the 1946 world champion Cardinals, catch the ceremonial first pitch from "the Man." As the story goes, Musial was unaware of the arrangement until the morning before and when he found out, he canceled his appearance.

A scrambling Cardinals front office secured Ozzie Smith to make the first pitch. Ironic, because "the Wizard" is part of the other great feud in Cardinals history—his beef with Tony La Russa.

There's nothing to be done about the Musial–Garagiola feud. Musial died in January 2013 and took it with him.

But there is still hope, faint as it may be, to patch things up between Smith and La Russa. The dispute developed during spring training in 1996. Smith was coming off a difficult 1995 season in which injuries had limited him to 44 games and a .199 batting average. He also turned 41 years of age over the winter as he entered the final year of his contract.

Understandably concerned, the Cardinals traded three pitchers— Allen Watson, Rich DeLucia, and Doug Creek—to San Francisco for 26-year-old shortstop Royce Clayton. Obviously, they made that deal with the intention of making Clayton their first-team shortstop and easing Smith into a part-time role.

Part of what made Smith great, if sometimes difficult to deal with in the late stages of his career, was his ego, the chip on his shoulder, an inner drive that told him no one could be better. He thrived on proving himself and proving others wrong.

For instance, in 1990, shortly after he succeeded Whitey Herzog as Cardinals manager, Joe Torre sent a pinch-hitter to the plate for Smith. Incensed, Smith tore off his jersey and went directly to the clubhouse. Torre told a clubhouse attendant to get Smith, but Ozzie refused to take a spot on the bench until Torre had the attendant return and inform Smith he would be fined $1,000 for every inning he didn't watch from the dugout.

But we digress.

When La Russa publicly stated the starting shortstop job would be an open competition during spring training '96, Smith took him literally.

When spring training was over, the bottom line showed Smith batting .288 with no errors and Clayton batting .190 with eight errors. As far as Smith was concerned, the open competition was a closed case. He had to be the winner. But when the season started on April 1 in New York, Clayton was the starting shortstop.

Smith was livid. La Russa explained that the numbers did not tell the whole story in terms of who played the position more dynamically.

"I think it's fair to say he misunderstood how he compared to Royce in spring training," La Russa said. "When I and the coaches evaluated the play in spring training—the whole game—Royce started very slowly offensively and you could see him start to get better. By what he was able to do defensively and on the bases, Royce deserved to play the majority of the games."

Smith cried foul, and pulled no punches in doing so:

"You know he's not doing what the man said he would do," Smith told reporters. "Anyone who sits down and listens knows it's a lie. It's things like that that don't allow you to have respect for people. That's cowardice, as far as I'm concerned. But should I expect anything different?

"It wasn't so much about my playing time as the way it was done. I was under the impression I was going to have every opportunity to do what I do. I was told that the position would be earned in spring training. And I thought I did that. I did everything that was asked of me."

And with that, the Hall of Fame shortstop and Hall of Fame skipper have been at odds ever since. Smith would have little to do with the club as long as La Russa was around. Since TLR retired with one last championship in 2011, Smith has been an instructor at each spring training and a regular in Cardinals functions.

When La Russa was elected to the National Baseball Hall of Fame Museum in 2014, along with fellow manager Torre and Bobby Cox, it meant Smith had played for four Cardinals managers who were Hall of Fame members—Herzog, Red Schoendienst (interim in 1990), Torre, and La Russa.

But there was one with whom he still had no relationship.

"I've always admired Joe Torre and Bobby Cox," Smith said at the time. "The other guy (La Russa)...uh, I never really knew him."

Where the middle ground is, hard to say. One can understand the point of view of a prideful athlete. One also can understand La Russa was trying to create a competitive environment in spring training and get the best out of his players, as he was wont to do.

And if you read between the lines, it's not hard to imagine a 26-year-old Clayton was covering more ground than a 41-year-old Smith. Herzog once explained it in a different manner:

"Ozzie always helped me. I could bring him in my office and tell him what I wanted done, and he'd do it. I'd say, 'Tell this guy I want it done this way, or he'd find himself on the wood.' Ozzie liked that. He liked being the king.

"He was the ultimate showman. He'd make two diving plays a night that would make the crowd go crazy. It started to make me wonder. I'm thinking, 'If Ozzie is making two diving plays a night, how come you never see anybody else ever diving?' You realize, 'That's Ozzie.'"

So how would you persuade Smith to let bygones be bygones? Perhaps if he considered one other bottom line, besides those spring training statistics.

Clayton batted .277 with a .312 OBP and .692 OPS in 129 games in 1996. One-and-a-half seasons later, he was traded to the Texas Rangers.

Starting roughly one game a series in 1996, Smith stayed relatively healthy and finished his career in style. He batted .282 with a .358 on-base percentage and a .728 on-base-plus-slugging percentage in 82 games, among the best marks of his career. Five years later, he was elected to the Hall of Fame.

La Russa managed 15 more seasons for the Cardinals, had several more shortstops, and in 2013 was elected into the Hall of Fame.

Smith won, La Russa won, and it all came out in the wash. Don't take it to your grave, Ozzie; life's too short.

Own a 1994 Fleer Pro-Visions No. 5 Ozzie Smith Baseball Card

Although there were a few scattered baseball trading cards in production during the 1860s and 1870s, used in advertisement and promotional campaigns, the first mass-produced, nationally distributed baseball cards began showing up in the mid-1880s.

Goodwin & Co. Tobacco Company in New York issued the Old Judge cards, a small card inserted into packs of Old Judge brand tobacco. Other tobacco companies then followed suit and there were well over 2,000 cards produced during the era.

Some are among the most highly sought after by collectors, the most valuable cards in the industry. Some cards, like Yum Yum tobacco, S.H. Hess, and Four Base Hits, are extremely rare and quite expensive. Most of the insert cards are much smaller than the cards made today.

The 1880s series featured the likes of Cap Anson, Mike 'King' Kelly, Buck Ewing, and Charles Comiskey.

In the early 1900s the U.S. government successfully sued to break up the American Tobacco Company monopoly. With the splintering of this group into smaller independent companies, cards once again became a viable way to promote tobacco products. The period from 1909 to 1915 is regarded by many as the golden age of baseball cards. Tobacco and candy companies produced some of the most beautiful, original, and valuable cards of all time.

Examples from this era include the T206 White Borders series, produced from 1909 to 1911 and sold in various packs of cigarette brands. The set includes the T206 Honus Wagner card, the holy grail of baseball cards, the collector's dream.

The Honus Wagner card was removed early during the printing production and experts believe there are about 50 to 100 of the cards in existence. A 1909 T206 Honus Wagner in top condition fetched $2.1 million at auction in 2013. Arizona Diamondbacks owner Ken Kendrick paid $2.8 million for a particularly desirable version of the card in 2007.

Perhaps you could afford to own the card someday. Perhaps that's on another bucket list.

But if Honus Wagner claims the most valuable card in history, Cardinals Hall of Fame shortstop Ozzie Smith might just lay claim to the most unusual card in history.

The Fleer Pro-Visions illustrated line of cards was a bit out there to begin with, no question. For instance, the 1993 Tom Glavine card shows the lefthander making a pitch while his right foot is placed on a sheet of ice, with an ice skate on and a hockey net behind him. And that's just part of the picture.

The '94 Pro-Visions version for Smith leans heavily on a *The Wizard of Oz* theme, depicting Smith in a wizard's red robe and hat, decorated in stars. There is a Cardinal bird on his right shoulder and he appears to be standing on the infamous Yellow Brick Road, with what appears to the Land of Oz and the Emerald City itself in the distant background.

Smith appears to be juggling six baseballs, wearing his Rawlings Trapeze glove on his left hand. In a nod to accuracy, Smith does have his left index finger sticking out the back of the glove, which is the way he normally wore his mitt.

Ultimately, art is in the eye of the beholder. Or perhaps in this case, the collector. Certainly, the unusual drawing makes for a unique card and while it does not come close to matching the Honus Wagner card in value, the Ozzie Smith card does have a Wagner reference. On the flip side, the card states:

Going into the 1993 season, Osborne Earl Smith had been chosen as the NL's top fielding shortstop 13 times in a row. The "Wizard of Oz's" peerless acrobatic skill with leather is universally recognized. What's not well recognized is Smith's proficiency with the stick and on the basepaths. For 16 consecutive seasons, Smith has swiped at least 20 bases. Since 1900, only Honus Wagner has equaled that feat. At the plate, Smith has turned into a remarkably smart and savvy batsman, perfect for the patented motion offense of the Cardinals. The All-Universe shortstop is one of just 12 players to accumulate 2,000 hits and 500 steals in a career."

Smith finished with 16 seasons of 20 steals or more, three fewer than Wagner. "The Wizard" wound up with 2,460 hits and 580 steals. "The Flying Dutchman" had 3,420 hits and 723 steals.

That said, Wagner's 1909 card says little more than "Piedmont" and "The Cigarette of Quality" on the backside.

So, come on. One is all colorful with interesting baseball information on the back. The other is much smaller, has no information, and is worth around $3 million.

I mean, really, which would you rather have?

- -

Join Redbird Nation

WHERE: On the Cardinals' website (www.cardinals.com), click on the "Fans" icon.

WHEN: Whenever the mood strikes you

WHAT TO DO: Complete the Redbird Nation order form at www .cardinals.com/redbirdnation. You must provide complete and accurate information, including name, address, telephone number (e.g. home, work, mobile, and fax), email address, valid payment card information, and shipping address. The Cardinals.com Privacy Policy explains how such information may be collected and used. The email address used at purchase or activation will be your Redbird Nation member login.

COST: As of 2015, the price was $19.95. At the end of each season, a membership can be renewed at the original fee.

BUCKET RANK: 🪣

- -

Most of us have heard the term "nation building," certainly where it applies to world events. The conventional use of the term might describe endeavors that include peacekeeping, humanitarian assistance, counterterrorism, and counterinsurgency. These actions are usually taken with the mission of organizing a state and creating order inside another country.

That said, the Cardinals engage in their own form of nation building. They are constructing a Redbird Nation, and they want you and everyone you know to get on board. And in this case, with all due respect to those who categorically reject the idea of nation building, it's not a bad gig.

Joining Redbird Nation isn't just rewarding in a prideful, self-indulgent sense. It comes with some decent perks. A new member of the club receives an identification card to carry in his or her wallet, clearly identifying him or her as a pennant-waving enthusiast and staunch supporter of Cardinals baseball. What's more, new members who joined in 2015 qualified for the following swag:

- Two tickets to a regular season 2015 Cardinals home game (via voucher code to be redeemed online)

- 2015 MLB.com® Gameday Audio for your computer

- 10% off entire purchase coupon for the St. Louis Cardinals Team Store (some exclusions may apply)

- 10% off entire purchase coupon for the Cardinals.com Online Shop (some exclusions may apply)

- Buy-One-Get-One-Free Busch Stadium Tour coupon

- Access to select presales and exclusive ticket discount offers throughout the 2015 season

- Special offers related to merchandise and more

- Special access to Redbird Nation members-only pages

- Exclusive club message board

By the way, the season-long subscription to MLB.com Gameday Audio allows you to listen to all 2,430 regular season games live, or on demand with no blackouts. You can choose home, away, or alternate audio (where available) to keep up with the Cardinals wherever they are.

Just imagine 2,430 regular season games. That's 15 seasons' worth of baseball packed into one summer. That's 21,870 innings, give or take some extra innings. Anyone who can listen to that much baseball should not only be in Redbird Nation, she should be institutionalized.

Keep in mind you also can give a Redbird Nation membership as a gift, which means, in effect, you can do some nation building of your own.

Purchase a Personalized Brick at Busch Stadium

WHERE: The sidewalks outside Busch Stadium III

WHEN: TBD

WHAT TO DO: Wait for the club to offer more bricks. A total of 10,158 square feet of pavement was covered with the bricks as Busch Stadium III was built. Another area for bricks will need to be added, or time and deterioration will offer more opportunities.

COST: Previous prices were $155, $305, and $360, but the bricks sold out.

BUCKET RANK: 🪣🪣🪣🪣🪣

We've all seen our share of masonry. Anyone who saw Ozzie Canseco patrol the outfield in 13 games for the Cardinals in 1992–93 knows what hands of stone look like. But did you know you could own some of the masonry outside Busch Stadium? Well, you can. Or, that is, you could.

Cardinals fans have a powerful connection to their team. A father stands with his sons as they view a brick dedicated to his late wife outside of Busch Stadium.

Starting in November 2004, the club began offering commemorative bricks for sale. The engraved objects are located on the east and west sides of the ballpark, surrounding the 100 engraved granite pavers that commemorate the Cardinals' greatest moments.

Interspersed with each other are standard 4x8-inch bricks, which carry personal messages, and more elaborate 8x8-inch bricks, which include "child art" creations with drawings or more elaborate displays.

The problem, in terms of this bucket list, is that the bricks sold out in 2006 and as of early 2016, the club has not offered more. But keep a stout heart. Where there is profit to be made, there is hope.

Certainly, one might make perusing the existing bricks a bucket-list item. The messages left on the mortar can be as entertaining and diverse as the fans behind them. Some are funny, some motivational, some introspective and emotional.

Some people bought the bricks as a means to remember or honor loved ones, some to thank the Cardinals or favorite players for years of enjoyment, and some to memorialize a special event or person in their lives.

Many bricks employ the signature expressions of Cardinals' broadcasters, such as Jack Buck's famous "That's a winner" call and his description of Ozzie Smith's playoff home run in 1985, "Go crazy folks! Go crazy!" Mike Shannon is well represented with "Old Abner has done it again," and "Get up, baby, get up!"

Other messages lean less on cliché and more on commitment. At least one brick poses a romantic question: "Will you marry me?" Somewhere among the sea of red mortar there might be an answer.

One fan used a popular promotional teaser: "Hot dog $3.50. Cold beer $7.50. Watching the Cards beat the Cubs—priceless." Another fan honored a loved one by saying, "In memory of Greg Farris, He cheers from his seat above."

Meanwhile, a married couple remembered their vows by buying a brick with the inscription, "Right here, our life as 1 began. Forever, we will be Redbird fans."

There were some restrictions in place for language and sentiments conveyed. Some bricks were rejected by the Cardinals' screening team, including a submission by a die-hard Boston Red Sox fan.

Those who purchased bricks were also shipped a duplicate brick for their own keepsake. The personalized brick program has been a popular vehicle for raising money at a number of the newer sports facilities. The company that installed the Cardinals' program, Fund Raisers Ltd. of Boise, Idaho, was involved in similar drives at Coors Field in Colorado, PNC Park in Pittsburgh, the Great American Ballpark in Cincinnati, and SBC Park in San Francisco, now AT&T Park.

More recently, the St. Louis Blues hockey team followed suit, beginning a personalized brick program for the Scottrade Center in 2014.

A portion of the proceeds from the Busch Stadium brick sales were directed to the team's charitable affiliate, Cardinals Care. But club chairman Bill DeWitt Jr. acknowledged the donation was a relatively small percentage of the revenue generated. Most of the money was used to defray the cost of the construction of the stadium, which opened to a Cardinals World Series title in 2006.

"We didn't want to focus on [Cardinals Care] too much, " DeWitt said at one point. Thus, fans who ordered the bricks were not allowed to claim the expenditure as a charitable donation…sorry, Charlie.

For out-of-town Cardinals fans who made brick purchases, half the fun is coming to a game at Busch Stadium and finding their own brick. The Cardinals, of course, provide a directory of where bricks are located.

One of the more compelling bricks reads, "Many thanks to the great fans! So, Emiko, and Kan Taguchi #99."

That piece of ballpark immortality was purchased by Cardinals outfielder So Taguchi, the first Japanese player to wear the Birds on the Bat. A fan favorite, Taguchi was with the club during the transition to the new stadium and for parts of six seasons (2002–2007). Taguchi played on two World Series qualifiers (2004, 2006) and a world championship winner (2006).

His homer off Mets reliever Billy Wagner in Game 2 of the 2006 NLCS helped propel the Cardinals to a World Series and remains among the more memorable blows in franchise history. He remains the only player ever to wear No. 99 for the club. He batted .283 in 578 games as a Cardinal.

And as the brick suggests, he cherished every moment.

Donate to Cardinals Care

The Cardinals Care program was founded in 1997 and has provided cash grants to children's organizations and founded a flagship youth baseball program—Redbird Rookies. The program provides more than 4,500 St. Louis–area kids a chance to play baseball and learn life lessons along the way. Cardinals Care has also built or revived 22 baseball fields in and around the St. Louis area.

The most recent of those ballfields to be dedicated was Tony La Russa Field, which opened for play at Ray Leisure Park, 1410 South Tucker Boulevard, in May 2015 just south of downtown St. Louis. Although he was working for the Arizona Diamondbacks at the time, La Russa was on hand for the ceremony.

He also talked about his own childhood experience and what the field meant to him.

"When I grew up and I had a chance to play a lot, I did not have anything as nice as this, " La Russa said. "There was no grass in the infield; there were rocks. We had bruises. So this is—this is beautiful."

Tony La Russa Field is typical of the detail the Cardinals put into the new fields, first class all the way. The field featured fresh sodding, fencing, scoreboard, a pitcher's mound, and plenty of bleachers.

The Cardinals Care director explained the field would become the hub to the Kingdom House and city recreation leagues, which included 24 teams.

Cardinals president Bill DeWitt III said the goal of Cardinals Care is to stretch "shallow and wide"—that is, support as many groups as possible through small, annual grants.

La Russa, the Cardinals' manager from 1996–2011, was a key contributor and supporter to the program during his stay. When Tony La Russa Field was dedicated, Cardinals chairman Bill DeWitt Jr. paid tribute to his former skipper's contribution.

"You supported [Cardinals Care] and helped make it what it is today," DeWitt said. "Given that we have already retired your number and inducted you into the Cardinals Hall of Fame, we felt there would be no more fitting tribute, an appropriate honor, than to name this field after you."

Among those attending the ceremony was 10-year-old Kennard Greenlee. He had been involved with the Redbird Rookies program since he was five years old and spoke to the crowd gathered about what it has meant to him.

"During my journey here, I have grown to better my character in the real world," said Greenlee. He then quoted the pioneering Jackie

The Cardinals Care program, founded in 1997, gives back to the St. Louis community by providing cash grants to children's organizations, building baseball fields, and more. In 2012, Cardinals President Bill DeWitt presented a check for $20,000 to the Ronald McDonald House to rebuild homes lost in the May 2012 tornado in Joplin, Missouri.

Robinson: "A life is not important except in the impact it has on other lives."

The biggest fundraising vehicle for Cardinals Care is the annual "Winter Warmup." The three-day fan festival in downtown St. Louis features appearances by numerous current and former players and in 2015 raised more than $700,000. But you don't have to attend the Winter Warmup to be part of the program that supports so many children's organizations. You can donate from home.

Donors can make a tax-deductible contribution to Cardinals Care and, if they choose, make the donation on behalf of, in honor of, or in memory of an individual, company, or group. An acknowledgment card is sent to the honoree and all donors receive notification of their donation.

You can donate by check, payable to Cardinals Care, and mail to: Cardinals Care, 700 Clark Street, St. Louis, MO 63102. Or go to www. stlcardinals.com, click on "Community," scroll to the bottom of the page, and click on "Donate to Cardinals Care." It will guide you through the process.

As for those looking for support, the Cardinals Care program is happy to help nonprofit groups and fund-raising efforts through donations whenever possible. Because of the high volume of requests it receives, it asks those inquiring to follow guidelines and provide, at minimum, eight weeks' advance notice.

Here are some of the other youth baseball fields the program has constructed include around St. Louis:

All-Star Field
St. Louis, Missouri
(Herbert Hoover Boys Club)

PAL Memorial Park
Fox Park
St. Louis, Missouri
(Police Athletic League)
Funded by Darryl Kile

Lou Brock Field
St. Louis, Missouri

Edgar Renteria Field
East St. Louis, Illinois
Jackie Joyner-Kersee Center

Jack Buck Field
University City, Missouri

Red Schoendienst Field
Normandy, Missouri

Cardinals Care Field
Hamilton Heights

Ozzie Smith Field
St. Louis, Missouri
(Vashon High School)

Jim Edmonds Field
Adams Park (SE Forest Park)

Spirit Field
Spanish Lake, Missouri
(For disabled wheelchair play)

Bob Gibson Field
St. Louis, Missouri
(City Recreation)

Woody Williams Field
Northwoods, Missouri

Whitey Herzog Field
Belleville, Illinois

Mark McGwire Field
Forest Park, St. Louis, Missouri

Heine Meine Field
Lemay, Missouri

Sesser Field
Sesser, Illinois

Stan Musial Field
Jennings, Missouri

Yadier Molina Field
Wellston, Missouri

Chapter 2

Things to Read

Read A Well-Paid Slave: Curt Flood's Fight for Free Agency in Professional Sports

In August 2015, Curt Flood was inducted into the Cardinals Hall of Fame Museum in a ceremony at Ballpark Village. During the ceremony, Flood's former outfield running mate Lou Brock addressed the large gathering and thanked the Hall of Fame for "welcoming Curt Flood back home to be with us."

That's a sentiment that is often lost in Curt Flood's epic battle against baseball's reserve clause. In large part, Flood wasn't fighting for the right go somewhere else. He was fighting to stay.

Flood was a terrific player for the Cardinals, an instinctive center fielder who might have made his way to Cooperstown had his career not been interrupted. Over 12 seasons in St. Louis, he batted over .300 six times and was a catalyst for a team that won three pennants and two world championships. He had a .293 average overall for those seasons and won a series of seven Gold Gloves, at a time when Willie Mays was patrolling center field for the San Francisco Giants.

During one stretch, Flood played in 226 consecutive games without committing an error, and in 1966 he went the entire season without a misplay.

But in 1968, he misplayed a ball that cost the Cardinals dearly in the seventh game of a World Series loss to the Detroit Tigers. And the following season, the two-time National League champs finished fourth. Ownership decided it was time to remake the roster and Flood was dealt in a trade with Philadelphia that brought slugger Dick Allen to St. Louis.

Flood was devastated, and soon after he was informed of the trade he sent Commissioner Bowie Kuhn a letter saying he wouldn't go. He would sue baseball. According to the reserve clause rules at the time, if he would not sign a contract for the Phillies he would have to effectively retire. And at age 31, in the prime of his baseball life, he effectively did.

Over the next three years, Flood took the fight to Kuhn and Major League Baseball, with players' union head Marvin Miller as his *consiglieri*. The original case wound up being heard by Judge Irving Ben Cooper in the Federal Court of the Southern District of New York. Flood lost, but he kept going.

The Supreme Court elected to hear Flood's argument with a trial that commenced in 1972. In a 5–3 ruling, the Court found against Flood on the basis of *stare decisis*, adhering to the principles established in the previous ruling. One of the justices refused to comment because he held large stock in Anheuser-Busch, which owned the Cardinals at the time.

I think that's called *protectus your own interestis.*

The author of *A Well-Paid Slave*, Brad Snyder, is a lawyer by trade and the heart of the book focuses on the heart of the matter. As he was at times a terrific leadoff man for the Cardinals during his career, Flood's battle was the leadoff spark that set wheels in motion for the successful challenges of players Andy Messermith and Dave McNally in 1975.

Free agency became a reality that now sees the major league minimum at more than $500,000 and the average salary in 2015 at $4.25 million. Oh yeah, and players still get $100.50 per day in meal money on the road.

At one point during the affair, Flood appeared on television with celebrated commentator Howard Cosell.

"It's been written, Curt, that you're a man who makes $90,000 a year, which isn't exactly slave wages." Cosell said. "What's your retort to that?"

Flood responded: "A well-paid slave is nonetheless a slave."

Hence the name of the book. But there is more to Flood than meets the legal pad—much more.

He grew up in Oakland, playing baseball for George Powles, the same white coach who was a mentor to Frank Robinson and basketball's Bill Russell. Flood signed in 1956 with the Cincinnati Reds, where his experiences with segregation would harden him for the road ahead. Often, he was not allowed to eat at Southern restaurants where teammates dined. He was barred from one visitors' clubhouse, and had to change clothes in a shed next to the dugout.

He was traded to the Cardinals in December 1957, where he bonded with black and white teammates alike, and enjoyed the best years of his life. Flood attempted to restart his career in Washington in 1971, while his legal skirmishes were still going on, but he was out of shape and out of sorts. The comeback ended just 13 games in.

Outside the lines, Flood was a complicated man, and not always an admirable one. He had big problems with alcohol and personal finances. He was an incorrigible womanizer and a negligent father to five children. He also scammed people into buying portraits that he signed but did not actually paint. During the 1970s, the stress and fallout of his legal battles sent him scurrying to Europe. He lived in Majorca, Spain, for five years, a self-imposed exile.

Flood returned to baseball briefly, when he became a broadcaster for the Oakland A's in 1978.

His scars and blemishes aside, he was charming and personable, a talented artist and musician, a highly intelligent and articulate man. Later in his life, he came to grips with his demons and his best qualities shone through. After a battle with throat cancer, Flood died in January 1997 at the age of 59.

Snyder touches on all of the elements that make Flood's story so compelling, while devoting a majority of the book to the pioneering legal battle. Snyder's writing style is thorough, but not especially entertaining. At times, the book reads more like a history textbook than a captivating tale. But it is the best of several manuscripts that have been spent on Flood.

Flood's selfless sacrifice of his outstanding playing career is something that has made an impact on all sports, something all of today's independently wealthy athletes should be aware of and grateful.

Flood isn't in the National Baseball Hall of Fame in Cooperstown, New York. Miller, the former players union executive, was by Flood's side through his epic legal war. He understood the parameters.

"There is no Hall of Fame for people like Curt," Miller once said.

Miller was wrong. There's a Hall of Fame in St. Louis for Curt Flood, where his journey has come full circle. As Brock suggested, No. 21 finally came home.

· ·

Read October 1964 by David Halberstam

There have been countless books written about baseball and quite a few that focus on the Cardinals or one of their many notable players. They are sometimes unoriginal in content, if not somewhat corny and predictable. But this is one of the best, printed by Random House Publishing in 1995 and a follow-up to Halberstam's previous best-selling work *Summer of '49*.

In *Summer of '49*, Halberstam focused on a more innocent age in America's national pastime, the start of the Casey Stengel years in New York, and a Yankees dynasty that lasted through the 1950s into

THE MOST REMARKABLE ASPECT OF BOB GIBSON'S 1.12 ERA

As David Halberstam profiles in his book *October 1964*, Bob Gibson was an emerging star in 1964. But the best was yet to come.

Gibson would win 20 games in 1965 and 21 in 1966, then return from an injury to beat the Red Sox three times in the 1967 World Series. But Gibson's signature season was 1968, a season he completed with a record low 1.12 earned run average.

For Tim McCarver, who was behind the plate for most of the 1,161 batters Gibson faced in '68, the most astounding number associated with that season is not 1.12. It's the number nine—that is, the number of games Gibson lost during that unparalleled summer.

"When I think of 1.12, that's the thing that stands out most about it to me," McCarver said. "How did that happen? I still don't know. He must have borrowed some losses from other seasons."

Time passes and the lowest ERA baseball had seen in 54 years remains the lowest it has known for 47 years since. More than 100 years of 1.12.

The '68 season is forever remembered as the Year of the Pitcher and the primary reason was the pitcher of the year. A 32-year-old Gibson was at the height of his considerable powers, a supreme athlete, a daunting figure, an uncompromising competitor.

Gibson's menacing aura is based in large part on perception. He never led his league in hit-by-pitch, never finished higher than third. He is not 12 feet tall. He is 6'1" and 187 pounds. He is not brusque or ill-tempered in person. He turns 81 this year and you might easily mistake him for a retired English teacher.

But as Halberstam underlined in his book, perception becomes reality. As No. 45, Gibson peered in with authority, uncoiled like a viper, and couldn't wait to get the ball back and do it again. He didn't retire opposing batters; he terminated them.

Old adversary and now close friend Dusty Baker says of him, "The only people I ever felt intimidated by in my whole life were Bob Gibson and my Daddy."

Gibson completed 28 of his 34 starts in 1968. During the six games he didn't finish, he came out for a pinch-hitter each time. His manager Red Schoendienst never went to the mound to get him, and why would he? Gibson's ERA in the eighth and ninth innings was 0.62.

His season included 268 strikeouts over 304.2 innings. It featured 13 shutouts and 24 starts in which he allowed one run or less. It left opposing hitters with a .184 batting average and .233 on-base percentage. It was a summer in which San Francisco's Juan Marichal led the National League in wins (26), complete games (30), and innings pitched (325.2).

But the Cy Young and MVP awards both went to Pack Robert Gibson. In his signature season, he was more than a pitcher. He was an American Sniper, and he didn't miss.

"Everybody talks about how violent his delivery was and how violent his pitches were, and that's all true," said McCarver, who also was a primary catcher for Hall of Fame pitcher Steve Carlton. "But to have that movement and violence in his pitches and combine that with control...it just doesn't happen.

"He could fit it in a little ball-and-a-half area, and he was there all the time. He didn't make any mistakes."

Gibson wasn't complicated. He threw two pitches: fastball and slider. If you were a hitter guessing along with him, you had a high probability of being correct. And yet you had no chance.

"While it's correct to say Bob just threw two pitches, it was in name only because those pitches did everything," McCarver said. "The action in the strike zone was by far the most vicious that I ever caught. So his fastball-slider served as many pitches because he didn't have an idea about where they were going until 1968.

"There's been many, many different combinations of how to get hitters out. But I defy anyone to say that any pitcher in the history of the game had the combination of power and control like Bob Gibson had in 1968."

During a stretch from June 6 through July 30, 1968, Gibson worked 99 innings and allowed three runs. One of the runs scored on a questionable wild pitch, another on a bloop double just inside the playing line. When the run started he was 5–5; when it ended he was 15–5.

He led the Cardinals to a pennant, then struck out 17 Detroit Tigers in Game 1 of the '68 World Series. The sight of burly Willie Horton buckling on the final strike remains burned into baseball's montage.

And when it was all done, when 1.12 was recorded, it didn't just boggle the mind. It changed the game. During the following winter, Major League governors instituted a new rule, lowering the height of the pitching mound from 15 inches to 10 inches.

"He changed the dimensions of the playing field," McCarver said. "I mean, Jim Brown didn't do that. Roger Maris didn't do that. Mark Spitz didn't do that. He changed the game, that's what 1.12 means."

By the way, Bob Gibson won 22 games during that 1968 season. It remains unclear how he lost nine.

the early 1960s. In *October 1964*, Halberstam picks up the story and focuses on the end of the Pinstripes' prominence, bringing it into context with the social changes and Civil Rights Movement taking place in the country.

The predominantly white Yankees, with aging stars like Whitey Ford and Mickey Mantle, represented a steadfast, antiquated status quo in America. Like most American League teams at the time, the Yankees had been slow to embrace baseball's integration, averse to scouting and signing African American players.

The 1964 Cardinals, on the other hand, epitomized a new climate that was gaining traction in the game and the country. The Cardinals were anchored by charismatic African American stars like Bob Gibson, Lou Brock, Curt Flood, and Bill White. The support group included veteran standouts such as Ken Boyer and Curt Simmons and was complemented by young stars like Tim McCarver and Ray Sadecki.

What's more, the eclectic, interracial group became a cohesive unit, developing professional and personal bonds that helped them capture an improbable pennant and upset baseball's established giant in a seven-game World Series.

The Pulitzer Prize–winning Halberstam, who died at age 73 in 2007, weaved all of these aspects and elements into a captivating historical tale: a baseball story at its core, a cultural and social examination in its entirety. Critics have argued—with some justification—that this symbolic turning point in baseball actually began a year earlier. The mighty Yankees were swept in the 1963 World Series by the Los Angeles Dodgers, a team that featured African American standouts such as Maury Wills, Willie Davis, John Roseboro, Jim Gilliam, and Tommy Davis.

Then again, the '63 Yankees lost to the Dodgers largely because of the incomparable pitching arms of white starters Sandy Koufax and Don Drysdale, and white closer Ron Perranoski. The Bronx Bombers scored just four runs in four games, losing to Koufax twice.

The '64 Yankees were beaten by World Series stars like Brock and Gibson, the likes of whom they had never seen, the likes of whom they avoided pursuing for their own roster. The only African American regular in the Yankees' lineup at the time was 35-year-old catcher Elston Howard.

It was one thing to strike out 15 times and lose to the superb Koufax. It was quite another to get fanned 13 times and be dominated by Gibson, an imposing African American right-hander.

Halberstam had a wonderful thirst for detail and an inexhaustible commitment to research. His ability to underscore team dynamics, identify moral romance, and disassemble staid stereotypes comes alive in sensitive, revealing portraits of players and managers, and makes the work most entertaining.

For instance, about Gibson he writes,

"Sometimes Gibson seemed to forget how imposing he was. He knew he was threatening on the mound—that was deliberate—but he had little sense that for many people he was unapproachable and distant off the mound. He hated small talk....He was a man who lifted an entire team. His own standards were so high that the other players did not like to let him down, and they played harder when he pitched.

"In time this became true on the other days as well. Years later, Steve Carlton, a pitcher who apprenticed on the Cardinals when Gibson was in his prime, would talk about how much he had learned from Gibson, which became critical to his making the Hall of Fame: the ability to focus on a game, the ability to be tough and, perhaps even more important, the ability to create a mystique of toughness."

Read Bob Gibson's Stranger to the Game

As they like to say in show business, Gibson needs no introduction. He is probably considered the greatest pitcher in Cardinals history, with a possible argument from Dizzy Dean. Gibson pitched for 17 years in the big leagues, with a 251–174 record and a 2.91 earned run average. He won as many as 20 games five times and won two National League Cy Young Awards (1968, 1970).

He is best known for two things—his record-setting 1.12 ERA in 1968, when he won both the Cy Young and the Most Valuable Player awards, and his World Series performances. Gibson was 7–2 with a 1.89 ERA in nine World Series starts. He struck out 92 in 81 innings, which included a record 17 strikeouts against the Detroit Tigers in Game 1 of the 1968 World Series.

Gibson was also known for casting a menacing figure on the mound, with his fiercely competitive nature and unforgiving attitude toward beating the opposition. Much of his career took place during times in which America and baseball were especially challenging places for an African American man, environments choked with bigotry and stunted by racial prejudice.

Gibson approached the world in much the same manner he approached an opposing hitter, which is reflected in his book. Through fascinating episodes and revealing vignettes, the book takes readers though Gibson's early childhood experiences with his older brother Josh, his time playing basketball with the Harlem Globetrotters, his caustic relationship with Cardinals manager Solly Hemus, the unusual bond he shared with the Cardinals of the 1960s, and his many remarkable performances.

At the same time, Gibson offers numerous examples and no-nonsense reflections on what his world was like and the sometimes painful situations he found himself in as an African American man, his athletic celebrity notwithstanding.

For instance, Gibson was the 1964 World Series MVP after leading the Cardinals to a dramatic seven-game win over the New York Yankees. But unlike the World Series MVP of the year before, white Dodgers left-hander Sandy Koufax, Gibson got almost no endorsement offers after winning his award.

"While Koufax was able to cash in nicely, the only thing I got out of my minor celebrity was a trip to the Rose Bowl," he writes.

Gibson was presented with a new Chevrolet Corvette as the World Series MVP. But his financial status at the time was so marginal, he wound up selling the car shortly after receiving it. He then explained that America at the time wasn't ready for a black man in a Corvette.

"My initial experience with the Corvette was a bad one anyway," Gibson writes. "Just after I got it, I was driving from St. Louis to Omaha when a policeman pulled me over in a small town in Missouri. He told me there was a report of a stolen Corvette that matched the description of the one I was driving. I said, 'Bullshit.'

"I knew he was just messing with me because he didn't believe that a black man could come by a Corvette honestly. When he asked to see the title papers I told him that I didn't have any yet because I had just won the car for being the Most Valuable Player in the World Series. He then apologized, which policemen and others tend to do when, and only when, they find out they're hassling a public figure.

"Through baseball, I was able to travel and circulate much more freely than the average black man, but even for me it was not uncommon for bigotry to come barging through."

Gibson also reveals the affection, respect, and admiration he had for so many of his teammates. That comes out most profoundly when he discusses center fielder Curt Flood and Game 7 of the 1968 World Series. Gibson had won seven consecutive World Series games as he took the mound on October 10, 1968, at Busch Stadium with the series tied 3–3.

He was deadlocked in a 0–0 standoff with Tigers left-hander Mickey Lolich after six innings. But with two on and two out in the bottom of the seventh, Detroit's Jim Northrup hit a drive to center field that Flood would normally gobble up. But the Cardinals' Gold Glove outfielder initially misjudged the ball, then lost his footing as he tried to recover. Northrup's shot went to the wall for a two-run triple and the Tigers went on to win the game 4–1 and the World Series. Lolich was the MVP, not Gibson.

At the time, and ever since, observers have assigned the goat horns to Flood for a misplay that popped Gibson's impenetrable bubble and cost the Cardinals another world championship. But Gibson offers a different perspective:

"A week later, I was in an airport somewhere when an old lady recognized me and walked up to say something," he writes. "I assumed she was going to ask for an autograph or maybe congratulate me for my season or my World Series records. Instead, she asked me if I still spoke to Curt Flood. "I said, 'Lady, how can you ask that?'

"The irritating absurdity of her question—the most regrettable aspect of the fact that Flood is still held accountable by many people for what happened in the seventh game—lies in the reality that Curt Flood was more than my best friend on the ballclub. To me, he personified what the Cardinals were all about. As a man, as a teammate, he was smart, funny, sensitive, and most of all unique. As a ballplayer, he was resourceful, dedicated, and very, very good. Hell, the little guy was us, through and through."

By the way, Gibson and Wheeler published a second book in October 2015: *Pitch by Pitch: My View of One Unforgettable Game.*

Read Tony La Russa's Books

For those who devour it, baseball is a game of endless possibilities and outcomes. The combination of nine ballplayers spread over a three-acre field, surrounding four bases, manipulating a ball nine-and-a-half inches in circumference has infatuated sports fans for well over a century.

The game is immediately accessible to those who care only about the rudiments—three outs, three strikes, four balls, nine innings. And it is forever captivating to those who embrace it more deeply, who ponder each situation and contingency, who study the myriad angles, who appreciate the rich history, who think along with the thinkers.

Buzz Bissinger's *Three Nights in August* appeals to every category of baseball fan, taking readers deep inside the obsessive mind of a Hall of Fame manager—Tony La Russa—while profiling many of the personalities and predicaments that touch on a long season.

Bissinger was given full access to the club and full cooperation from La Russa during the 2003 major league season. From the first day of spring training on, the author was in the manager's office, in team meetings and postgame assessments, at team dinners and parties…a veritable fly on the dugout wall as the Cardinals chased a National League Central Division crown.

The club finished 85–77 that season, three games behind the division-winning Chicago Cubs and two behind the second-place Houston Astros. The competition with the Cubs was especially meaningful, punctuated by the bat of Sammy Sosa and the electrifying young arms of Kerry Wood, Mark Prior, and Carlos Zambrano.

The Cubs were managed by Dusty Baker, who developed quite a feud with La Russa over his years in both Chicago and Cincinnati. In fact, the combative skippers engaged in a memorable exchange during an ensuing September series in Chicago.

For the purposes of *Three Nights in August*, the author homed in on the Cardinals' three-game homestand against the division-leading Cubs in late August. The Redbirds won two of three from the visitors, climbing from three games back to one game behind. More importantly, the rivalry presented a slice of baseball in its most delectable form, a series between two of the game's romantic adversaries, in the midst of a pennant race, infused with all the emotion, color, and history one could siphon from one weekend.

What Bissinger does best is profile La Russa, a man who rubbed players and fans every which way with his intensity, assertiveness, and extreme dedication to preparation and detail.

"Every successful manager has players," La Russa once said. "That's the No. 1 message. Coaches and managers don't decide baseball. Players decide it. But what you do as a coach or coaching staff is you have a responsibility and opportunity to help put the players in their best position to compete."

No one spent more sleepless nights or restless hours fretting the results and no one embraced the process more than La Russa.

As a player, he would be the first to tell you his career was mostly forgettable. A top prospect coming out of high school in Tampa, Florida, he hurt his arm playing in a softball game and never found big-league traction. He spent bits and pieces of six seasons in the big leagues as an infielder with three different teams. He had 176 at-bats, 35 hits, and a .199 career average.

As a manager, however, his career took him to Cooperstown.

La Russa was just 34, the youngest manager at the time, when he was hired by Bill Veeck to manage the Chicago White Sox in 1979. Over the next 33 years, he would compile a 2,728–2,365 (.536) record, winning the World Series with the Oakland A's in 1989 and with the Cardinals in 2006 and 2011. He also guided the White Sox to an American League Championship Series (1983) over eight seasons, the A's to three AL pennants (1988–90) over 10 seasons, and the Cardinals to three NL pennants (2004, 2006 and 2011) over 16 years.

When he retired after leading the Cardinals to a title in 2011, La Russa had the most managerial wins (1,408) in Cardinals history and his overall total ranks third among big-league managers. Only Connie Mack (3,731) and John McGraw (2,763) won more games than La Russa.

Three Nights in August opens a window into what made La Russa special, the close working relationship he had with pitching coach Dave Duncan, and the numerous considerations that went into his decision making. It also reveals much about La Russa off the field, his self-doubts, his appreciation for the history and traditions of baseball, and the way he handled all things affecting the game and the men who played for him.

Within that framework, the book spins off sidebars and anecdotes that had an impact on the 2003 team and the particular series. The emergence of slugger Albert Pujols, the stunning death of pitcher Darryl Kile in Chicago the previous season, and the Cinderella rise of infielder Bo Hart are among the revealing treatments. In the end, the book is an engrossing read for both the strategist and casual fan alike.

As a follow up, be sure to read *One Last Strike: Fifty Years in Baseball, Ten and a Half Games Back, and One Final Championship Season*. Penned with longtime Cardinals beat writer Rick Hummel, La Russa takes fans through the 2011 season and the storybook final chapter of his career.

Among the many behind-the-scenes insights, it explains how La Russa felt the Texas Rangers underestimated David Freese's ability to set his front foot quickly and drive pitches to the opposite field. That talent allowed Freese to famously tie Game 6 in the ninth inning with a two-out, opposite-field triple, then win it in the 11th with a home run to center field.

La Russa explains: "I didn't think the Rangers had a good read on Freese's opposite field power and how his ball would carry that way. If they had, [outfielder Nelson Cruz] might have been positioned deeper. If Cruz had recognized it, he might have broken back more quickly. Whether human nature factored into this at all, them being one strike away, I can't say."

In *One Last Strike*, La Russa takes fans step by step through his final journey that led to a championship and his decision to make it his last season as a manager.

Chapter 3

Places to Go

Attend Cardinals Spring Training

WHERE: Roger Dean Stadium, 4751 Main Street, Jupiter, FL 33458. Call 561-775-1818.

WHEN: Grapefruit League games normally begin in March and end the first week of April.

WHAT TO DO: Keep an eye out for the release of the Cardinals spring training schedule for the coming year, which usually happens in mid-November of the current year. Pick out dates and start making plans to visit Jupiter, Florida, and see the Cardinals play in spring training.

COST: Travel costs will vary, of course, depending on whether you fly or drive and where you're coming from. The following quoted hotel prices were listed for mid-March 2016, which will be the middle of spring training. In 2015, reserved seats for Cardinals spring training games at Roger Dean Stadium were $40 for box seats, $30 for reserved, $15 for bleachers, $15 for berm (lawn seats), and $10 for standing room. On the weekends, the prices go up between $2 and $5.

BUCKET RANK: 🪣🪣🪣🪣🪣

* * *

If you're a baseball fan—no, a real baseball fan—you would love spring training. It's not the quality of the baseball, per se. Frankly, with nothing on the line or ultimately on the record, the baseball can have a rec-league feel to it, especially early in the Grapefruit League season. With 6,000 in the stands instead of 46,000, there is a discernible lack of excitement—just lots of substitutions, lots of unfamiliar names, and lots of forgettable innings.

Fans who attended Spring Training in 2015 were lucky enough to get an advance look at rookie phenom Stephen Piscotty, pictured here in a March exhibition game against the Miami Marlins in Jupiter, Florida, before he broke out in the 2015 season. Piscotty was called up to the majors in the summer of 2015 and was a crucial component of the Cardinals' postseason run.

That said, it's major league baseball in a charming hybrid form. There is usually a spot or two open on the big-league roster or the pitching staff, and a handful of players being considered. It can be intriguing to track the competition and speculate on the decisions.

It's also a chance to see a new regular acquired during the off-season or an exciting prospect. Often, a spring-training phenom emerges, capturing the imagination and causing managers to rethink their blueprint.

In essence, spring training presents the game on a smaller, exploratory scale, and in cozier environs. Mix in a clean slate, a fresh dose of optimism, and the soothing properties of the Florida sun, and you have a surefire cure for cabin fever. For players, coaches, and fans alike, it is much more of a hands-on experience.

The closest airport to Roger Dean Stadium is Palm Beach International, about 20 miles from Jupiter proper. Major airlines go into Palm Beach, including American, Delta, Southwest, and United. Also consider flying into Fort Lauderdale or Miami, where fares can be significantly cheaper. Miami International Airport is 84 miles from Roger Dean Stadium. Fort Lauderdale Airport is 67 miles away, so it can be worth the relatively short drive.

You have a lot of choices of hotels. Some are more convenient than others, some more pricey than others. For instance, the new Courtyard Palm Beach Jupiter ($359 a night) is right across the street from Roger Dean Stadium. You can roll out of bed and into your seats. Other popular hotels, such as Homewood Suites by Hilton Palm Beach Gardens ($211), DoubleTree by Hilton Hotel Palm Beach Gardens ($279), Jupiter Beach Resort & Spa ($411), and PGA National Resort & Spa ($379) require a short drive. There are many other options, so check around.

Roger Dean Stadium (www.rogerdeanstadium.com), which opened in 1998, is located at 4751 Main Street, Jupiter, FL 33458. Both the Florida Turnpike (exit 116) and I-95 (exit 87) run parallel to Jupiter at Indiantown Road, making either road convenient to access Roger Dean Stadium off exit 83 (Donald Ross Road).

As noted above, tickets for Cardinals spring training games can be difficult to come by, depending on your arrangements and the opposition. All ticket windows, including "Will Call," are located adjacent to the main entrance gate behind home plate. The ticket office opens at 9:00 AM, but the line often starts forming around 7:00 AM. Gates open two hours before the game. Parking is $5 per vehicle in a grass lot just northwest of the field.

Given the berm seats are sold on a "day of game" basis, there are always seats available. But tickets are best purchased in advance, which can be accomplished at the Cardinals' website (www stlouis .cardinals.mlb.com) or at Roger Dean Stadium by calling 561-775-1818. The Cardinals' dugout is on the first-base side. To sit on that side of the stadium, buy tickets in sections 101–113 or 201–207.

The berm, by the way, is a grassy area located by the Cardinals' bullpen down the right-field line with a capacity of 200. It's a great spot for kids, just a handshake's distance away from the players seated in the bullpen.

There are opportunities to ask for autographs and interact with the players between innings. But keep a couple of things in mind. First, these guys are working, so they may prefer to sign after the game or between workouts. Also, a foul ball can come sizzling into that area so it's important to pay attention when the game is on. The area is intended for children, so ushers use their discretion in discouraging patrons if they start driving the players nuts.

Otherwise, you can line up before and after workouts and games to ask for autographs. There is a trolley that transports fans through the complex and out to the back fields to watch training during workout days and before games. The workouts are free and open to the public.

That said, fans enjoy a little better access on the Marlins' side of the complex, where all the practice areas are accessible. On the Cardinals' side, fans are allowed to watch at Fields 1 and 6. Players and fans often walk through the same areas in the Marlins' complex, but not so much on the Cardinals side. One thing both sides have in common is bleachers that are set up at accessible fields.

Roger Dean Stadium is part of a planned community and located in the heart of the Abacoa Town Center, which is open for lunch daily at 11:00 AM. There is a Starbucks nearby for the early birds (so to speak). Four main bars/restaurants are in the immediate complex, including Rooney's, Jumby Bay Island Grill, JJ Muggs Stadium Grill, and Masa Sagami (a Japanese steakhouse). There are also lots of other things to do while you're there, like going to the beach, playing golf, fishing, and shopping in opulent West Palm Beach.

SPRING TRAINING PHENOMS

If you attend spring training, you'll want to keep your eye out for the spring training phenoms. They arrive each March, wherever major league teams gather. They open eyes, confuse general managers, and make even the most knowledgeable fans drool.

They often come unsung and unexpected, but they soon become undeniable with each sizzling line drive.

In spring training 1965, the Cardinals were the reigning world champions. Their lineup was set in stone, anchored by 1964 National League MVP Ken Boyer, who played third base and batted cleanup. There was no place to put another third baseman...or was there?

Young Ed Spiezio had batted .360 at Tulsa the previous summer, enough to secure a cup of coffee in big-league camp, a meet-and-greet in St. Petersburg, Florida. Management had no intention of keeping the Joliet, Illinois, native and no place to put him.

But as general manager Bob Howsam put it that March, "How are you going to tell a young fellow he needs to go down and learn more about his trade when nobody can get him out?"

Spiezio went off, so much so that an April 1965 *Sports Illustrated* story featured him under the headline, "Please, please, Ed Spiezio, won't you please pop up?"

By the time the grapefruits were ripe and the Cardinals were headed north, the 23-year-old was batting a nifty Florida .515. That's not an average; that's a mandate. The Birds on the Bus had no choice but to bring Spiezio with them.

But, as often happens when a regular season begins, when the games count and the pressure mounts, the spring training excitement gives way to a sobering major league reality. Spiezio, indeed, started popping up.

"It's really tough to judge players in March and September," former Cardinals manager Whitey Herzog said. "You'll call someone up in September, when they're not trying to make a ballclub and they don't have much pressure on them, and they'll play great.

"Then they come to spring training and a lot of them get tight now that they're really trying to make the ballclub. But it works both ways. Sometimes they'll play like hell in spring training, then the regular season starts and the pressure and everything...they tighten up. It's hard to know that's going to happen."

Once the Cardinals opened the '65 season, Spiezio batted .167 in 10 games. Before you could say "spring phenom," he was on a flight to Class AAA Jacksonville. In the end, due in part to a string of injuries, Spiezio never became the player that 1965 spring suggested he might.

He was a part of three pennant winners in St. Louis, so no condolences required. What's more, his son Scott became a valuable member of the 2006 world champion Cardinals, batting .272 with 13 home runs off the bench, contributing a memorable pair of two-run triples in the National League Championship Series.

But over five seasons with the Cardinals, Ed Spiezio never found that spring swing. He played in just 132 games and batted .205. The story epitomizes the bait-and-switch properties a phenomenal spring training can have.

"There is something to say about it," said Lee Thomas, a former director of player development for the Cardinals and former general manager for the Philadelphia Phillies. "That's where you have to be really be careful because spring training can fool you.

"Bing [Devine, former Cards general manager] used to tell me, 'Don't let people fool you in spring training.' But it happens, happens all the time."

But it doesn't happen *every* time. In the spring of 2001, the Cardinals promoted Albert Pujols to their Grapefruit surroundings. Pujols was the 402nd player taken in the 1999 draft and had just one season of professional baseball to his credit, spent mostly at Class A Peoria.

During a late-season promotion to Class AAA Memphis in 2000, he pushed the accelerator, batting .367 in the Pacific Coast League playoffs. His reward was a look in Jupiter, Florida, and he made the most of it. Still considered a raw commodity, he was issued jersey No. 68 and bounced around to five different positions. But he batted .306 with three home runs and forced management to pay attention.

"Each week when we had our cut meetings, there we were, figuring he had to go back to the minors at some point, and each week he kept impressing us more and more," former Cardinals general manager Walt Jocketty said. "It got to the final week and we just said, 'Look, we're a better club with him,' the way he was playing."

Pujols stuck and didn't stop. He went on to become the National League Rookie of the Year and finished fourth in MVP balloting with a .329 batting average, 37 home runs, and 130 runs batted in. He even got a more appropriate number to wear—No. 5.

The impression Pujols made in the spring of 2001 was a precursor to what could be a Hall of Fame career. He has not been quite the same player since signing with the Los Angeles Angels. But from 2001 to 2011, Pujols played 11 seasons in St. Louis, collecting 445 home runs, 1,329 RBIs, and a .328 batting average.

Turns out he wasn't just a spring fling.

If you hope to bump into players when you're out and about, nightspots to consider are the Waterway Cafe at 2300 PGA Boulevard and Abbey Road Grill and Raw Bar at 10800 Military Trail in Palm Beach Gardens. Nick's Tomatoe Pie at 1697 W. Indiantown Road in Jupiter is another favorite for dinner.

The Cardinals will be training at Jupiter for the 19th spring in 2016; they previously trained across the state in St. Petersburg. One of the charms of spring training is the opportunity to visit other ballparks and see other teams. That was easier when the Cardinals were in St. Pete, with some seven teams around them. You have to be ambitious and adventurous to do a lot of that from Jupiter.

EXTRA POINTS

Five Memorable Cardinal Spring Phenoms

Ed Spiezio
Hit .515 in 1965 spring training
Hit .205 over five seasons with Cards

Jim Lindeman
Has eight HRs in 1987 spring training
Batted .208 with eight HRs in full 1987 season

Khalil Greene
Hit .408 in 2009 spring training
Batted .200 in regular season

Albert Pujols
Hit .306 with three HRs in 2001 spring training
2001 NL Rookie of the Year, .329 37 HRs, 130 RBIs

Kip Wells
Pitched 23 innings, 1.16 earned run average and 22 strikeouts in 2007 spring training
Finished 7–17 with 5.70 ERA in 2007 regular season.

It would be wise to check when the Cardinals play as the visiting team at other spring training sites (Mets, Nationals, Braves) as well, in case you are vacationing in other parts of Florida. Also check to see when they play as the visiting team at the Roger Dean Stadium complex, which they share with the Miami Marlins. It can be easier to get tickets to see the team play on the road, and when they play the Marlins, the only difference is the color of the uniforms and the order in which the teams bat.

At www.floridagrapefruitleague.com, you can check out the schedule for the Cardinals and all of the other teams playing on the spring training circuit.

The New York Mets train in Port St. Lucie, which is only a 35-minute drive. But the next closest team is the Washington Nationals in Viera, Florida, about one-and-a-half hours away. The Houston Astros camp in Kissimmee, Florida, is some two hours' drive from Jupiter. The Atlanta Braves are in Lake Buena Vista, which is some 20 minutes farther.

As mentioned, a boatload of teams are still on the west side of Florida, if you want to bounce around.

If you're going to make a week of it in Florida and attend two or three games, the stay is going to be somewhere in the $2,000–$4,000 range, depending on how extravagant you care to get. However, there are attractive spring training packages available that include travel and accommodations, along with game tickets and some amenities. They vary in length, but are generally less than $2,000 per person based on double-occupancy. Consult the Cardinals (www.stlouis.cardinals.mlb.com; 1-800-892-7687, Altair Travel & Cruises (www.altairtravel.com; 314-968-9600 or Sunrise Tours (www.travelsunrise.com or 314-771-8300 for more details. Also check with the various Jupiter-area hotels about special packages being offered in association with spring training.

Meet Someone at the Stan Musial Statue

WHERE: The statue is in Stan Musial Plaza outside the main entrance, on the third-base side of Busch Stadium, 322 South 8th Street (at Spruce Street) in St. Louis, MO 63102

WHEN: Usually before or after a Cardinals game, but if you're visiting St. Louis, any old time will do

WHAT TO DO: Make arrangements with a friend or group of friends to meet at the Stan Musial statue outside the ballpark

COST: An open mind

BUCKET RANK: 🪣

M eeting at the Stan Musial statue has become a tradition for Cardinals fans, if not pigeons, since the statue was dedicated on August 4, 1968, at old Busch Stadium. Besides the Gateway Arch on the riverfront, it is the city's most significant piece of sculpture and a tribute to its most chivalric sports hero.

The statue sits on a black granite base, where the words of baseball Commissioner Ford Frick are engraved: "Here stands baseball's perfect warrior. Here stands baseball's perfect knight." Frick made the comments while speaking during a ceremony honoring Musial before his last game on September 29, 1963.

Musial is universally considered the greatest Cardinal. His Hall of Fame career included three National League MVP awards, 24 All-Star Game appearances, seven batting titles, 475 home runs, 3,630 career hits, and a lifetime batting average of .331. Moreover, Stan "the

Meeting at the Stan Musial statue has become a tradition for Cardinals fans since it was dedicated in 1968. Musial himself, however, was not completely keen on the interpretation of his likeness. (Jasen Vinlove-USA TODAY Sports)

MUSIAL

Man" was widely beloved for his wholesome lifestyle, generosity, and gentlemanly demeanor.

With his various business ventures in town, his association with the organization, and his contributions to countless charities and community programs, Musial was the face of the franchise and the heart and soul of the city for some 70 years.

That said, the sculpture is somewhat less revered. The bronze likeness of Musial, crouched in his stance, holding a bat, is 10'5" tall and stands atop a granite base that is an additional 8'6" in height. Longtime *Post-Dispatch* sportswriter Bob Broeg spearheaded the idea for the tribute, gaining the support of the local chapter of the Baseball Writers Association of America.

But the group had an entirely different concept in mind. Upon Musial's retirement in 1963, *Post-Dispatch* artist Amadee Wohlschlaeger presented the legendary player with a painting titled *The Boy and the Man...Baseball's Bond*. Wohlschlaeger, who created the newspaper's iconic "Weatherbird" and also drew the sports figures on the backs of Raisin Bran cereal boxes, depicted Musial signing an autograph for a young boy. The original painting now hangs in the Cardinals Hall of Fame at Ballpark Village.

Broeg and his constituents voted to adopt the painting as the model for the sculpture. Broeg even wrote a column announcing the plan, presenting an artistic rendering of the approved proposal. But when the BBWAA contributions came up some $10,000 short of the $40,000 price tag, St. Louis mayor Raymond Tucker stepped in. He passed the project to Carl Mose, a friend and modernist sculptor on the staff of Washington University.

As one figure was cheaper than two, Mose designed a new concept, intent on capturing an individual Musial in his famous batting stance.

But Mose's interpretation presents Musial with especially large shoulders, holding a relatively tiny bat and standing much too square and erect. In real life, Musial's unconventional batting stance was fluid, elastic, almost wistful. In modernist form, it is heavy, mechanical, and warriorlike.

Musial was never one to speak badly of someone but even he was disappointed in *Musial*.

"He'd made me all bulky," Musial said shortly after the statue was completed. "I tried to get him to change it, but he just never would. So finally I told him, 'Well, just go on and get it done.' He never did get it right."

For his part, Mose accepted the criticism matter of factually. He reportedly told an interviewer that a sculptor's work is like that of a baseball umpire, "always open for criticism, particularly from the subject, his relatives or friends...that's the risk you take."

The controversy notwithstanding, Musial was obviously moved at the dedication and choked up as he declared, "I want to thank everyone—for my mother and the Musial family—for making me a Cardinal forever."

Whether you like the artistic statement it makes or not, the statue certainly has made Musial a Cardinal forever. Its presence and staying power were never more evident than when Musial passed away on January 19, 2013, at the age of 92. The street alongside the Musial Plaza became impassable. People gathered at the statue to leave stuffed animals, flowers, photographs, memories, and prayers.

Among them was 84-year-old Joe Fleming, who had been a visiting batboy when Musial was at the Class D affiliate in Williamson, West Virginia. In 1939. The young Musial was a left-handed pitcher at the time, which was before he hurt his arm and became a prolific hitter.

Later in life, Fleming moved to St. Louis and encountered Musial—by then a legend—outside the ballpark one day. He reminded Musial that he knew him way back when.

"He could not have been more gracious," Fleming recalled. "To me, Stan will always be the St. Louis Cardinals. He loved the organization. He loved the city. He loved the people. And they loved him."

Also part of the impromptu memorial to Musial that day was Robert Cradock. It was Cradock's company that made the granite foundation on which the statue stands. Cradock shared the amazing story that the statue was actually ready for dedication in 1966. But when the final sculpture model was sent to Mexico to be bronzed, it became lost.

Upon completing its work, the company in Mexico erroneously shipped the piece to St. Louis, Pennsylvania. By the time the mistake was discovered, the statue was found stored in a warehouse in eastern Pennsylvania. The bat was badly bent, Musial's elbow had been pushed out of position, and the bronze finish had been scraped off in a couple of places.

Stan Musial needed considerable restoration. But to do the work, the repairman had to be blindfolded and lifted into position because he was afraid of heights. Thus, the statue was not dedicated until '68.

"What I'll remember is simply how Stan liked people," Cradock said. "He found time for everybody."

Now every Cardinals fan finds time to visit the Stan Musial statue.

Visit the Real Stan Musial Statue in Springfield, Missouri

WHERE: Missouri Sports Hall of Fame, 3861 E. Stan Musial Drive, Springfield, MO 65809. The statue is in the "Legends Walk of Fame," a plaza adjacent to the main building.

WHEN: The museum is open Monday–Saturday, 10:00 AM to 4:00 PM; Sunday 12:00 pm to 4:00 pm.

WHAT TO DO: Visit the Missouri Sports Hall of Fame (417-889-3100 or 1-800-498-5678), see the statue and other exhibits

COST: Looking at the statue is free. To go in the museum, admission is $5 for adults, $4 for seniors, and $3 for children 6–15 years of age.

BUCKET RANK: 🪣🪣🪣

Y ou know what they say: if you can't build a Stan Musial statue right the first time...try, try again.

Four decades after Carl Mose unveiled his controversial statue of Stan Musial, the original design for the project was completed and now greets visitors to the Missouri Sports Hall of Fame in Springfield, Missouri.

The statue, titled *The Man and the Boy*, is based on a painting *Post-Dispatch* artist Amadee Wohlschlaeger presented to Musial upon his retirement in 1963. Wohlschlaeger, who also created the iconic

"Weatherbird" for the *Post-Dispatch* among his many credits, called the painting "the best thing I ever did."

Wohlschlaeger's original work is entitled *The Boy and the Man…. Baseball's Bond*. *Post-Dispatch* sportswriter Bob Broeg and the St. Louis chapter of the BBWAA voted to adopt the painting as the model for a Musial statue outside Busch Stadium. The painting depicts Musial leaning on his bat, signing an autograph for a wide-eyed young boy.

However, that idea fell by the wayside. Much to the chagrin of Broeg's group, as well as Musial's disenchantment, Mose changed the design and sculpted a singular figure of Musial in his batting stance. The finished product was dedicated in 1968.

Although controversial in its acceptance, the statue has become a St. Louis landmark and stands in Musial Plaza outside Gate 3 at the stadium today.

But in 2004, Missouri Sports Hall of Fame president Jerald L. Andrews got the idea to resurrect the original project. Hotelier John Q. Hammons provided $100,000 and artist Harry Weber was secured to sculpt Wohlschlaeger's concept for the Springfield museum.

There was a natural connection. Musial played in Springfield in 1941, a member of the Cardinals' Class C affiliate in the Western Association. In 87 games, he batted .379 with 27 doubles, 10 triples, and 26 home runs. That alone is worth a statue.

For his part, Weber has created a number of statues for Cardinals greats, including an additional Musial figure. His pieces are displayed at the corner of Clark and Eighth streets, outside the Cardinals' team store at Busch Stadium.

That collection includes Hall of Fame inductees Enos Slaughter, Dizzy Dean, Rogers Hornsby, Red Schoendienst, Lou Brock, Bob Gibson, and Ozzie Smith; former St. Louis Browns player and Hall of Fame inductee George Sisler; former Negro League St. Louis Stars player and Hall of Fame inductee Cool Papa Bell; and former Cardinals radio broadcaster and Hall of Fame honoree Jack Buck.

Each is shown in a signature action pose, sliding into home plate, making a diving catch, and the like. Musial is among them, following through on one of his memorable swings.

During his *The Man and the Boy* project, Weber invited Musial to his studio in Foristell, Missouri, to get input. Musial, 83 at the time, suggested several changes, a tuck here, a tweak there. As he studied the work, Musial observed Weber's rendition had the player signing a baseball for the boy. He took exception.

"You've got me autographing a ball," he told Weber. "Back in those days, they didn't have many balls being signed."

Weber countered, "Well, I got an autograph on a ball when I was a kid. Red Schoendienst autographed a ball for me. And that was in the '50s."

But Musial shook his head. He knew Weber's family was well-to-do, knew the sculptor was from a privileged upbringing. "You were rich enough to be able to get hold of a baseball," Musial said to Weber. "Most kids had pads or scorecards."

Weber made the change, taking the ball away and replacing it with a notepad. Instantly, the boy became the kind of scruffy, ordinary kid Musial had signed autographs for throughout his career.

Musial nodded his approval. "The old-time players took care of the fans," he said. "We promoted the game."

To thank Weber, Musial then asked the artist to hand him the clay bat from the sculpture and "the Man" signed one more time: "Stan Musial, H.O.F. 1969."

Weber's statue was dedicated outside the Missouri Sports Hall of Fame on April 2, 2005. Musial was in attendance and addressed the crowd:

"I want to compliment the statue for this reason: Red Schoendienst and I back in St. Louis, we parked our cars across from the baseball field. On the weekends, a lot of out-of-town folks had their children at the game.

"Red Schoendienst and I would sign at least for two hours for youngsters. We took care of the youngsters. We loved the fans. We loved baseball. When I see all the kids out here today, I appreciate all their enthusiasm."

Later that day, Musial threw out the first pitch as Springfield debuted its first Cardinals affiliate in 63 years at Hammons Field, a new $32 million downtown ballpark. It is believed to be Musial's last visit to Springfield before he died in January 2013.

. . . .

Visit Ballpark Village

WHERE: Adjacent to Busch Stadium, 601 Clark Avenue, St. Louis, MO 63102; 314-345-9481

WHEN: Before and after Cardinals games, or regular business hours, seven days a week

WHAT TO DO: Spend time in the Cardinals' new entertainment complex outside the ballpark

COST: Ballpark Village doesn't charge a cover, but some of its tenants do. Visitors under the age of 18 must be accompanied by a parent or guardian. And after 9:00 PM, all guests must be 21 years old or older with an ID. On non-game days, parking at Ballpark Village is free (with validation) for lunch and $2 (with validation) for dinner. On game days, hourly event rates will apply.

BUCKET RANK: 🪣🪣

. . . .

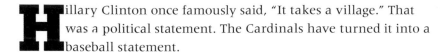

Hillary Clinton once famously said, "It takes a village." That was a political statement. The Cardinals have turned it into a baseball statement.

Long in the making, on the footprint of the former Busch Stadium, Cardinals owners finally filled the void with Ballpark Village, a $650 million project that opened for business in its initial phase in 2014.

Located just outside the left-field area of the stadium, the dining and entertainment district has been a huge hit, becoming almost one with the ballpark experience. Cardinals fans, in effect, have become Village People...cue the "YMCA" track.

Ballpark Village sits along Clark Avenue, covering ten acres and seven city blocks with retail shops, bars, restaurants, bars, entertainment venues, bars, grandstands, bars, 450,000 square feet of office space... and did we mention there are some bars?

The ballpark extension embraces and re-creates the all-inclusive, neighborhood experience baseball fans get when they attend a game at Fenway Park in Boston or Wrigley Field in Chicago. The Village, of course, is open year-round and caters to lots of other sports and entertainment events.

But it thrives before, during, and after the 81 regular season home dates and postseason games.

The first phase of Ballpark Village is anchored by Cardinals Nation, Budweiser Brew House, Fox Sports Midwest Live!, PBR St. Louis—A Cowboy Bar, Howl at the Moon, and Drunken Fish. There also is the Fudgery and Ted Drewes Frozen Custard, for the seamheads with a sweet tooth.

Five live-performance stages are incorporated on the grounds, which are covered by the largest retractable roof of its kind, the biggest indoor TV screen in the Midwest, and outdoor festival space that includes the original infield of the previous Busch Stadium, preserved in its exact historical location and dimensions. So if you never had

Ballpark Village opened in March 2014 and has become an entertainment hub for Cardinals fans ever since. The Busch 2 Infield gives fans a chance to walk the sacred ground once trod upon by legends.

the opportunity to field a ground ball at old Busch Memorial, it's not too late!

Cardinals Nation is of particular interest to baseball enthusiasts. The baseball commonwealth contains 34,000 square feet and four levels, featuring a two-story Cardinals Nation Restaurant & Bar, an

8,000-square-foot Cardinals Hall of Fame and Museum, a Cardinals Authentics Shop, selling game-used memorabilia, and the AT&T Rooftop.

The rooftop offers a two-story rooftop deck of 336 seats overlooking Busch Stadium. The spectacular views and all-inclusive experience are similar to what you might find on the rooftops outside Wrigley Field in Chicago.

In the Cardinals' dynamic pricing system, individual tickets to the AT&T Rooftop run between $70 and $150, depending on dates and opponents. The seats include an all-you-can-eat buffet that features a nacho bar, carvery, hot dogs, brats, additional entrees, action station, panini, salads, and desserts. Ticket holders also enjoy exclusive access to the indoor private dining area, full-service bar, private restrooms, and complimentary admission to the Cardinals Hall of Fame and Museum before and during the game.

In terms of seeing the game, Ballpark Village creates two other options. The second floor of Cardinals Nation features the Cardinals Nation Balcony, with views of what's happening inside the stadium. Tickets are priced similarly to the AT&T Rooftop and include similar amenities. The balcony seats are sold in tables of four and accommodate up to 12.

Then there is the Branch Rickey Room, a private room that accommodates 22 to 30 people, featuring a balcony with ballpark views and similar amenities to those aforementioned.

Budweiser Brew House sprawls across three floors of Ballpark Village and includes a beer garden and a rooftop deck, which also has a view into Busch Stadium. An extensive menu features steaks, seafood, and ribs. Meanwhile, the brews are represented by 239 taps, with suggested beer pairings to the menu. The actual ground-up beer bottles incorporated into the décor are worth seeing.

The heart of Ballpark Village is the central gathering place, known as Fox Sports Midwest Live! The area in the middle of the indoor complex is 20,000 square feet of entertainment marketplace, featuring a massive audio visual presentation, including a 40-foot-diagonal LED screen above a stage. Under a 100-foot-long retractable glass roof is a stage to host live concerts and events like the Cardinals Hall of Fame induction ceremonies. Also featured are a 200-seat restaurant and VIP seating area to enjoy the big game.

FOX Sports Midwest, the television home of the Cardinals, operates its studio on the second level overlooking FOX Sports Midwest Live! FOX Sports Midwest produces more than 200 shows per year at the studio, which looks directly into Busch Stadium from behind the anchor desk.

Country-and-Western fans will especially enjoy PBR St. Louis. Many of us are full of bull, but not many of us have actually ridden a bull. You can give it a go on the mechanical bruiser inside the cowboy-colored environment. The small concert club inside PBR St. Louis—the Barn—has kind of a campfire feel, backed by a stage in front of a stone fireplace.

After an initial stink over proposed guidelines, Ballpark Village doesn't have a dress code. But individual establishments might have restrictions.

Bottom line: wear your Miguel Mejia No. 35 jersey and you'll be fine.

Visit the Cardinals Hall of Fame Museum

WHERE: Ballpark Village, 601 Clark Avenue, St. Louis, MO—the museum is located on the second floor of Cardinals Nation

WHEN: Monday–Sunday, 10:00 AM to 6:00 PM. For more information, call (314) 345-9880 or go to www.stlballparkvillage.com/dining/play/cardinals-hall-of-fame-museum#sthash.nSNjui7c.dpuf

WHAT TO DO: Soak in the history and pageantry of baseball in St. Louis

COST: There is no door charge to Ballpark Village. Admission to the Hall of Fame is $12 for adults, $10 for senior/military, and $8 for children (under 3 are free). Admission is free with AT&T Rooftop tickets.

BUCKET RANK: 🪣🪣

Not everyone can get to Cooperstown, New York, to visit the National Baseball Hall of Fame Museum. But if you are able to get to Ballpark Village in downtown St. Louis, the Cardinals Hall of Fame is a worthy pinch-hitter.

It has a similar feel—the same manufacturer, Matthews International, was used to make the bronze plaques—and a similarly inspiring impact. The Hall of Fame opened in 2014 and for a variety of reasons, no ceremony was conducted for the initial 22 members. They are players who either had their numbers retired by the Cardinals or were already in Cooperstown.

But an annual induction ceremony is held to celebrate each additional class of inductees. In 2014, the first group of new honorees included Jim Edmonds, Willie McGee, Mike Shannon, and Marty Marion. In 2015, Ted Simmons, Curt Flood, Bob Forsch, and George Kissell joined them. Admission to the induction ceremony, which is held on the Cardinals Nation stage at Ballpark Village, is free, so there might not be a better time to see both Ballpark Village and the Cardinals Hall of Fame.

You will see a grizzled veteran catcher like Ted Simmons wax poetically about being a Cardinals Hall of Fame Player.

"There are really four organizations—the Dodgers, the Giants, the Yankees, and the Cardinals," Simmons said. "Everybody else kind of participates, if you know what I mean. This is a very special thing and not something people should take lightly. With the inclusions already walking around in this thing already, this is pretty humbling stuff."

Few franchises in baseball have the pedigree and tradition the Cardinals bring to the table, and their 8,000-square-foot museum on the second floor of Cardinals Nation reflects it. Featuring stadiums, players, and championship moments, the Hall of Fame has the largest team-held collection in baseball and is second only to the National Baseball Hall of Fame in scope, with more than 16,000 items of memorabilia and hundreds of thousands of archival photographs.

Pieces of a proud baseball heritage more than 100 years old are reflected in the jerseys, diamonds, press pins, and World Series trophies. Watch the opening film in the Sportsman's Park Theater and a lump will be stuck in your throat for the rest of the visit.

The museum is divided into sections and the highlights are too many to list. Take your time; there is lots to see, touch, hear, and experience. You can enter a broadcast booth, watch the replay of a dramatic moment in the past, and try your hand at doing the play-by-play.

You can put on Ozzie Smith's glove, or hold Stan Musial's bat. You can see the 1926 contract of Rogers Hornsby, which stipulates he was to be paid $30,000 "for his skilled services during the playing season of 1926 including World Series or any other official series in which the club may participate."

The Cardinals' World Series trophies are on display in the rotunda; when visitors stand in the center of the room, it is as if they are reduced in size and standing in the middle of a World Series trophy. In the Look of the Cardinals section you can go through the years with the iconic Cardinals jersey and how it has changed.

For the record, the birds appear on the bat for the first time in 1922. The jerseys are adorned, of course, with magical names, like Grover Cleveland Alexander and Dizzy Dean. There is even a reminder that Red Schoendienst once wore No. 6 before giving it back to Musial when "the Man" returned from the war. And David Freese's 2011 jersey is a little worse for wear...but that's what happens when you hit a game-winning home run in the World Series.

Special galleries are devoted to themed exhibitions rotating year to year that highlight special anniversaries, exclusive stories, and unique items in the team's collection. For instance, Red Schoendienst's game-used bat, the trophy ball from Red's 1,000[th] managerial win, and George Kissell's game-worn "Victory Blue" road jersey; Orlando Cepeda's 1967 National League MVP Award and 1967 world championship black bat; and 1967 Lou Brock's game-worn jacket, Bob Gibson's game-used helmet liner and batting helmet, and Chris Carpenter's game-used batting helmet.

And there's plenty more where all of that came from. Given the Cardinals have been to the postseason in 12 of the past 16 years, they won't be running out of new material anytime soon.

Sit in the Cardinals Club Seats for a Game

WHERE: Busch Stadium III, 700 Clark Avenue, St. Louis, MO 63102

WHEN: During a Cardinals home game

WHAT TO DO: Go to ticket-purchasing websites and find Cardinals Club premium seats for a game at Busch Stadium. Check several outlets to make sure you don't overpay.

COST: The price will be whatever the market will bear, so it might depend on the desirability of the game. But generally speaking, the Cardinals Club seats go for about $250 per game, or slightly less than the major league minimum salary of $507,500.

BUCKET RANK: 🪣🪣🪣🪣

This isn't exactly the Knothole Gang experience we're talking about here. No one is hopping on a Redbird Express, riding the bus to the ballpark, and paying a few bucks to sit in the grandstands.

No, this is how you go to a Cardinals game if money is no object. This is where you actually need to stop and check yourself in the mirror before you leave for the ballpark. This is sitting in the "front row," the seats directly behind home plate, with the screen in your vision and the sun on your face.

This is the Holy Grail of seat charts, God's Country, and for many, maybe a once-in-a-lifetime proposal.

SIT IN THE BLEACHERS

Nothing is the way it used to be, including the bleachers. Sitting just beyond the outfield walls used to be among the cheapest ways to attend a game. Bleacher seats went on sale the day of the game and seating was first-come, first-served.

Now the outfield bleachers at most ballparks, including Busch Stadium, are sold as both season tickets and individual-game tickets. The front rows of the bleachers at Busch, where the view of the game and the sound of your best heckling are unobstructed, are the most desirable and therefore the most expensive.

The bleachers, of course, present a different view of the action—that is, a view from the outfield perimeter in. You get an idea of what outfielders are looking at when a fly ball approaches. But there are drawbacks.

On a hot, sunny day, the bleachers are not for the faint of heart or sensitive of skin. There is no shade and no respite from the searing sun on a suffocating St. Louis summer day. Sitting in the bleachers for a Sunday-afternoon Cardinals game, on a sunny, 90-degree St. Louis day in July, is considered by some in the torture community to be just this side of waterboarding. A person could lose 10 pounds, depending on intake of concessions.

That said, there's something about sitting in the bleachers, something basic and authentic, whether the "right field sucks, left field sucks" chants breaks out or not.

For one thing, it is a prime opportunity to catch a home run ball. It is best to be located on the center-field side of the bleachers for this purpose. The visiting bullpen in left field and the Cardinals' bullpen in right both cut into the bleacher areas and tend to be a landing area for quite a few homers.

However, the occasional blast will transcend the bullpen and fly into the seats beyond—particularly if it is struck by Randal Grichuk. The Cardinals rookie hit a 448-foot homer at Busch in 2015.

The Cardinals' bullpen is located just beneath sections 107–109 in right field. Thus, the lower bleacher sections in 101–105 are most accessible to souvenir. The visitor's bullpen is beneath sections 189–191 in left field, making the lower seats in 183–187 most desirable.

FYI: prior to the 2015 season, the numbers for these sections were in the 500s (e.g., 591 instead of 191), but they have now been renumbered to be in the 100s.

The bleachers are bench-style seats. That is old school, but unlike in the old *days*, they do offer back support to allow fans to sit back rather than lean forward the entire game.

But it's complicated.

The seating chart for Busch identifies the Cardinals Club seats in sections 1 through 8 behind home plate. These babies are not available for purchase as individual game tickets or season tickets. All of these seats were sold in congruence with personal seat licenses upon the construction of Busch Stadium III. The acquisition of a PSL came with the obligation to buy season tickets for every year the St. Louis Cardinals play at the stadium.

If a Cardinals Club personal seat licensee fails to buy season tickets, said licensee loses said seat license and said seats, if you will. However, PSL owners can sell their tickets for individual games, which is why they become available through ticket-buying services.

Thus, on a given night, you can be a Cardinals Club ticket holder, which entitles you to the best seat in the house and all of the amenities. Among those delightful amenities is access to the Cardinals Club dining room and lounge, as well as VIP service throughout. That includes parking located right outside the stadium door.

You will want to arrive at the game early and bring an appetite. A buffet is served in the dining room before the game that usually includes four or five sides, featuring chicken, a fish dish, a meat-carving station, salad, soup, and desserts. Your drinks are included in the deal, whether you prefer soda, tea, beer, wine, cocktails, or frozen drinks.

When you get to your seats, the gluttonous adventure continues. There is also an "outside" menu, which includes things like bacon-wrapped hot dogs, toasted cannelloni, turkey wraps, and more. Beer, wine, soda, and water will be available, at your calling. You will have to get up to order a mixed drink or go to the bathroom. And the bathrooms are clean—no, really—with a polite bathroom attendant on hand. This is baseball—ballroom style.

And the fun doesn't have to stop when the ballgame is over, at least not immediately. The Cardinals Club bar stays open for an hour after each game, and remains open during all rain delays.

Oh yeah, did we mention a baseball game will be played?

Visit Grant's Farm

WHERE: 10501 Gravois Road, St. Louis, MO 63123

WHEN: During the summer months, the attraction is open from 9:00 AM to 3:30 PM Tuesday through Sunday, closed on Mondays. The schedule changes in the spring, fall, and winter seasons. There also are special Halloween hours. Call 314-843-1700.

WHAT TO DO: Take yourself, your family, or a group and enjoy a relaxing day.

COST: Admission to Grant's Farm, tram rides, and all shows are complimentary. A few attractions require a small fee ($2–$5) to participate. Parking is $12 per car and $30 per bus. A Season Parking Pass gives you unlimited access except for Grant's Farm evening events, including Halloween nights.

BUCKET RANK:

If you grew up in St. Louis, there is a good chance that you have been to Grant's Farm, which has been a field-trip staple for local elementary schools for many years. The property is a longstanding landmark and family attraction in south St. Louis County.

In 2012, the Zagat Survey ranked Grant's Farm as the seventh-best overall family attraction nationwide. The Zagat Survey and *Parenting* magazine surveyed more than 11,000 avid travelers to rate family-oriented attractions across the United States. So, in this case, batting seventh ain't bad.

The 281 acres of Grant's Farm land were gifted to Ulysses S. Grant and his bride Julia by his father-in-law, Frederick Dent, in the early

1850s. Grant, of course, later became a renowned Civil War general and 18th president of the United States.

At the turn of the 20th century, August Busch Sr. bought part of the original plot of land located some 11 miles south of downtown St. Louis. In the early 1900s, Busch used the property as a summer and weekend retreat. When Busch first began spending time at Grant's Farm, it was nearly a full day's carriage ride. Gravois was nothing more than a dirt road.

In 1907, construction began on the Bauernhof (German for "farmstead") and it was completed a few years later. The "Big House," which became the Busch family mansion, was completed in 1912. This is all historical background, and perhaps you are wondering where the Cardinals Bucket List connection is.

Stay close…we're getting there.

Among the residents, and later head of the ancestral estate, was August "Gussie" Busch Jr., who bought the St. Louis Cardinals from Fred Saigh in 1953. The brewery magnate, avid sportsman, and animal enthusiast was the principal and popular owner of the ballclub for more than 30 years, as well as six pennants and three world championships.

Upon Busch's death in 1989, the principal ownership of the Cardinals fell to Anheuser-Busch Cos., which was headed by August Busch III. "Three Sticks," who had ousted his father as head of the brewery in a corporate coup, did not share his pop's passion for baseball, and the Cardinals were sold to a group of investors headed by Bill DeWitt Jr. in 1996.

Twelve years later, in 2008, Anheuser-Busch was sold as well, purchased by the Belgium-based company InBev for $52 billion and change.

But we digress.

For many years, the Cardinals held their annual Pinch Hitters Ball-B-Que at Grant's Farm—and at 1963's event, Stan Musial officially announced his retirement from baseball. Today, visitors can interact with the famous Clydesdales.

In 1954, shortly after he bought the ballclub, "Gussie" Busch opened Grant's Farm to the public, and it has been operated as a popular family attraction ever since. The Busch family still owns Grant's Farm; AB-InBev owns the animals and pays to maintain the park. The historic grounds also contain a cabin called "Hardscrabble," built by Grant on another part of the property and relocated to the present site. It is the only remaining structure that was hand built by a U.S. president prior to his assuming office.

There are 1,000 animals representing six different continents and 100 different species at Grant's Farm. Visitors can ride a camel, feed a goat or parakeets, take a carousel ride, have a snow cone, or sample some of A-B's adult beverages at the historic Bauernhof.

But for Cardinals fans—and now we get to the reason for all the teasin'—the highlight has to be a visit to the official preparatory school for the world-famous Clydesdales.

The majestic creatures have become almost synonymous with Cardinals baseball, prancing through the wagon gates at Busch Stadium on Opening Day and circling the field to the Budweiser theme song, "Here Comes the King," advancing a tradition unlike any other.

Grant's Farm is home to more than 25 Clydesdales, who vary in age from 6 months to 15 years old.

A-B has one of the world's largest herds of Clydesdale horses and owns approximately 200 nationwide.

Frankly, it is a bit discriminatory in its practices.

If there were an Equal Employment Opportunity Commission representing Clydesdales, A-B no doubt would have some 'splaining to do. Only the finest of the breed become part of the Budweiser team, and the physical requirements are almost puritanical.

The perfect Budweiser Clydesdale must have the following traits:

- Full grown, the Clydesdale should stand 18 hands (about 6 feet) at the shoulder and weigh between 2,000 and 2,300 pounds. Sorry, no "plus" or "thin" sizes allowed.

- The horse should be bay in color, and have a blaze of white on its face, black mane, and black tail. White feathering on all four legs and feet is also required. If you're featherless, you need not apply.

- All the hitch horses are geldings, characterized by their even temperament and stronger, more natural draft horse appearance. In other words, be of stout mind and body.

Clydesdale Stables is located on the opposite side of the parking lot from the main entrance. You can check it out when you first arrive at Grant's Farm, before heading to the main gate, or as your final stop on the way out.

But if simply seeing the Clydesdale campus is not enough, there is a behind-the-scenes tour that provides a more in-depth examination of what it takes for these aspiring wagon pullers to make the grade and join the hitch—to be a Budweiser Clydesdale.

You will tour the remarkable stables and get an inside look at the entire Clydesdale operations, the actual training process, the daily maintenance—all things part and parcel of raising iconic horses. Tourists are welcome to bring cameras because they will be allowed to meet and interact with one of the retired hitch geldings.

This also answers the question that has been gnawing at many of us who have seen Opening Day at Busch Stadium. That is, what happens to a Clydesdale when he can't be a Clydesdale anymore, when he can't pull his weight (or the weight of the wagon), when the music stops? Well, he hangs out at Grant's Farm and poses for pictures with his biggest fans. In other words, it's hell gettin' old, unless you're a Clydesdale.

The walking Clydesdale tour lasts some 90 minutes, with portions taking place outdoors, off the paved path, so be prepared and dress accordingly. The cost for the tour is $25 per person.

MUSIAL'S ANNOUNCEMENT AT GRANT'S FARM

Grant's Farm is a lot of things: park, museum, zoo, conservation area, meeting center, and entertainment complex.

But it also has a unique place in Cardinals history. For many years, the team held its annual Pinch Hitters Ball-B-Que at Grant's Farm, where players and their families would mingle with fans in a barbeque setting, raising money for children's charities and socializing in an environment away from the ballpark.

It was in such an environment in late summer 1963 that Stan Musial officially announced his retirement from baseball. To give you the backstory, the 42-year-old Musial was in the midst of a 4-for-32 stretch in late July that season, and during a series in Milwaukee, General Manager Bing Devine called Musial and suggested the two meet for breakfast in Devine's hotel room.

Musial anticipated the topic of conversation might be his plans for the 1964 season. Between sips of coffee, "the Man" beat Devine to the punch. "After this year, Bing, I'll have had it," he said.

Musial told Devine he wanted to make the announcement in St. Louis and wanted to tell his teammates first. Devine suggested that a team picnic scheduled for August 12 would be an opportune occasion, and Musial agreed.

Two days later, Cubs left-hander Dick Ellsworth became the first (and only) pitcher ever to fan Musial three times in one game.

On a rainy Monday, August 12, the team picnic was held at Grant's Farm, the estate of Cardinals president Gussie Busch. Players, their families, team officials, and a small group of reporters were on hand. Busch was not in attendance, having left town for a family wedding. An emotional Musial stood in front of a bank of microphones and told the gathering he was calling it quits at the end of the season.

Cardinals shortstop Dick Groat remembers being stunned by the announcement.

"I didn't know anything about it until Stan announced it that night at the picnic," Groat said. "I felt disappointed and surprised. It was such a thrill to play with him. I really hadn't thought about his retiring."

When she got the news her son was retiring, Mary Musial sobbed uncontrollably. "I just couldn't believe it," she told a United Press International reporter. "Never to see Stan on the field again, 25 years gone just like that, I couldn't stop crying."

As he fought through his own tears, Musial delivered his speech. "Baseball has been my life," he said. "I love St. Louis and I've had fun all of these years."

He added the hope he might play in one more World Series. "I'd like to go out with a winner," Musial said. "Our '42 club was farther back."

The realization Musial was spending the last of his 22 years in uniform seemed to light a fire under the Cardinals. They were 64–53 and six games out of first place the day of Musial's announcement. But as September rolled in, the club reeled off 19 wins in 20 games.

"When he announced his retirement, it's like he woke everybody up on that ballclub," Groat said. "And I don't know what he hit from that day on, but he drove in one big run after another. He was just phenomenal."

Musial turned back the pages to bat .299 and drive in 12 runs during September. Most of his hits came in meaningful situations. As the Cardinals continued the surge, KMOX Radio executive Bob Hyland and trainer Bob Bauman conspired to dig out a copy of Spike Jones' "Pass the Biscuits Mirandy," the campy tune that became a clubhouse hit during the pennant runs of the 1942 and 1946 Cardinals. It became a hit all over again.

When the first-place Los Angeles Dodgers arrived for a three-game set from September 16 to 18, the retiring Musial and his team were one game back with 10 to play. They had won 10 in a row and 19 of 20.

In the first game of the series, the Dodgers led 1–0 behind the one-hit pitching of Johnny Podres when Musial batted in the seventh. On a 1–0 count, he pulled the 475th and final home run of his career onto the right field pavilion at old Busch Stadium (aka Sportsman's Park), knotting the score.

But the Dodgers scored twice in the ninth to snap the Cardinals' winning streak and take the series opener 3–1. The next night, Hall of Fame left-hander Sandy Koufax held the Cardinals hitless until Musial singled in the seventh. Koufax completed a four-hit shutout for his 24th win.

In the series finale, Musial had two hits as the Cardinals staked Bob Gibson to a 5–1 lead. But the Dodgers scored three in the eighth before Dick Nen's one-out homer in the ninth sent the game to extra innings. L.A. scored an unearned run in the 13th to win 6–5.

And just like that, the race was over.

The Cardinals lost three more in succession on their way to dropping eight of the last 10 and Musial's dream of one more World Series expired. Musial finished the '63 season with a .255 average in 379 at-bats. His 24 extra-base hits and 58 RBIs were the lowest totals of his career. For the first and only time in his career, Musial's strikeouts (43) exceeded his walks (35).

"I was even taking called third strikes, something I rarely did when I was younger," Musial said years later.

Although his career batting average on the road was .326, Musial batted .195 away from home during that final season. He still managed to bat .306 at home, with eight of his 12 home runs and 41 of his RBIs coming in 64 games at Grand and Dodier, where he played his entire career.

Musial's final farewell came on September 29, 1963. Pregame ceremonies lasted nearly an hour. Both the Cardinals and the visiting Cincinnati Reds lined the base paths, while dignitaries, friends, and family members sat in chairs beside a bank of microphones at home plate.

Cardinals captain Ken Boyer presented Musial with a gift from his teammates, a ring that contained the No. 6 set in diamonds. The Cub Scouts presented Musial a neckerchief, which he adorned and wore throughout the ceremony. Commissioner Ford Frick addressed the crowd of 27,576 and delivered a line that would later be inscribed on Musial's statue, "Here stands baseball's perfect warrior. Here stands baseball's perfect knight."

Owner August Busch Jr. told the crowd that No. 6 would never be worn again and Musial was presented with a framed likeness of a statue to be erected in his honor outside the new riverfront stadium. The design, titled *The Man and the Boy*, differed from the statue that was eventually dedicated. But it would be constructed years later and sit outside the Missouri Sports Hall of Fame in Springfield, Missouri.

Struggling with his emotions, rubbing his eyes, his hair, and his mouth to compose himself, Musial told the crowd, "This a day I'll always remember. This is a day of both great joy and sorrow...."

He thanked his wife and his children. He thanked God for giving him the ability to play baseball and last, his voice cracking, he thanked the fans. "I hate to say good-bye," Musial said. "So until we meet again, I want to thank you very much."

With his wife and family, Musial climbed into a convertible and rode in procession around the diamond he had occupied for so many years, waving to loud cheers and homemade signs. Finally, the Greatest Cardinal finished his career the same way he started it.

In his second at-bat, he singled past Reds rookie second baseman Pete Rose—who would break Musial's National League hits record. Then in the sixth, Musial pulled another pitch from 23-game winner Jim Maloney into right field for a run-scoring single, his 3,360th and final hit.

Manager Johnny Keane sent Gary Kolb in from the dugout to pinch run for Musial. At first the crowd jeered, not wanting Musial to leave. But as he headed to the dugout, Musial was sent off with one more emotional ovation.

He had gone 2-for-3 in a 3–2 victory, the same numbers that applied to his first Cardinals game. "I guess I never improved," Musial joked.

The afternoon proved painfully anticlimactic, lingering 14 innings before the Cardinals won. But for those who were there or watching on television, it remains unforgettable.

Musial compiled a profoundly symmetrical hitting career. He finished with 1,815 hits at home and 1,815 hits on the road. He hit 252 home runs at home, 223 away. He had 90 triples at home, 87 away; scored 999 runs at home, 950 away; stole 38 bases at home, 38 away; slugged .582 at home, .537 away.

He scored 1,949 runs and had 1,951 RBIs. Lifetime, he batted .323 or better in every month of the season. To this day, no major leaguer has had more hits in one uniform.

Although he only saw him play at the end of his career, the loquacious Bob Costas once summed up Musial astutely:

"He didn't hit a homer in his last at-bat (like Ted Williams); he hit a single. He didn't hit in 56 straight games. He married his high school sweetheart and stayed married to her, never married a Marilyn Monroe (like Joe DiMaggio). He didn't play with the sheer joy and style that goes alongside Willie Mays' name.

"None of those easy things are there to associate with Stan Musial. All Musial represents is more than two decades of sustained excellence and complete decency as a human being."

It will finish at the Label Stable gift shop, where you can purchase a piece of Clydesdale memorabilia.

And on your way out, go ahead; it's okay. You can hum the song. "Da da da da da da da ... da-da-da-dah!

. . . .

Attend the St. Louis Baseball Writers Awards Dinner

WHERE: Renaissance Grand Hotel, 800 Washington Avenue, St. Louis, MO 63101; 314-621-9600

WHEN: The dinner is normally conducted in mid-January.

WHAT TO DO: Purchase tickets. All seating is reserved and you can choose your table and seat by purchasing your tickets online. Go to www.stlouisbbwaa.com for all the information. Or you can mail a check to St. Louis Chapter BBWAA Charitable Foundation, P.O. Box 605, St. Louis, MO 63188. Call St. Louis BBWAA at 314-662-1701 for special dietary requests.

COST: Individual tickets were $150, while a table of 10 could be purchased for $1,500.

BONUS TIPS: Valet parking on Washington Ave. is $10, but it's only $5 for the hotel garage. If you have pull, you'll want to attend the VIP party, which is by invitation only and starts an hour before the dinner. Get there early to attend the general reception in the ballroom lobby.

BUCKET RANK: 🪣🪣🪣

. . . .

In 2016, the St. Louis chapter of the Baseball Writers Association of America conducted its 58th awards dinner at the Renaissance Grand St. Louis Hotel. The annual celebration of baseball in St. Lou is one of three surviving BBWAA awards dinners in the country—the others taking place in Boston and New York.

The BBWAA is a professional association of certified sports journalists founded in 1908. Originally, the organization was created to ensure professional working conditions for writers at all MLB ballparks and to impose a uniform method for scoring games.

The BBWAA once carried a significant amount of authority over admittance and activities in the press boxes. But in more recent years, it has lost quite a bit of its clout and now negotiates with MLB to preserve press-box integrity and encourage good working relationships with teams and players.

It's a standoff at best.

During its origins, the organization was made up almost entirely of beat writers and print journalists. Today, it includes contributors from a variety of accredited websites. As of 2014, the association counted 715 active members representing 26 major league cities.

To illustrate how things have changed, the original BBWAA was formed with 43 national members. The current association has approximately 100 international members, representing Canada, the Dominican Republic, Puerto Rico, Mexico, Japan, South Korea, and Taiwan. Some 600 members have voting privileges for the Hall of Fame ballot, including an estimated 40 from Canada and Japan.

From a fan's standpoint, the most significant function of BBWAA members—those with at least 10 years of tenure—is to elect qualified players to the National Baseball Hall of Fame and Museum. In addition, two voting members from each chapter vote in the selection process for MLB's annual awards—which include the Cy Young Award and MVP, Rookie of the Year, and Manager of the Year honors in the National and American Leagues.

So when the debate comes around about whether baseball's career hits leader, Pete Rose, should be in the Hall of Fame, or whether chemical enhancement has undermined the credibility of hall-of-fame candidates like Barry Bonds, Roger Clemens, or Mark McGwire, the BBWAA is the starting point.

And when one wonders why one's favorite Cardinals standout has not won a postseason award, or why Cardinals like Ken Boyer and Ted Simmons are not residing in Cooperstown, the BBWAA is your go-to target of angst and irritation.

That said, the local chapter puts on a heckuva dinner each January in St. Louis, a dinner where all things baseball and all things Cardinal are cherished, where reverence is bestowed on seasons past and fires are stoked for seasons to come. Portions of the funds raised by the dinner are used to make a variety of charitable donations in the community.

The first St. Louis BBWAA chapter dinner was staged in 1958 at the Sheraton Hotel. Legendary *St. Louis Post-Dispatch* scribe Bob Broeg was the catalyst behind the creation. While attending a BBWAA chapter dinner in Cleveland, it occurred to Broeg that St. Louis should have a similar affair to commemorate the BBWAA's 50th anniversary.

For the hook, the first dinner honored St. Louis baseball's All–Half Century Team, celebrating memorable players from both the Cardinals and the American League St. Louis Browns. The Brownies were still recently removed, having relocated to Baltimore after the 1953 season. Despite Broeg's late start in organizing the event, more than 1,000 people attended. A vein was tapped and a tradition was born.

With its many honorees and speeches, the inaugural dinner had dragged on well past midnight when baseball commissioner Ford Frick was introduced. Frick arose from his seat, stepped to the podium and delivered one of the most appreciated monologues in the history of the gala affair.

"Thank you, ladies and gentlemen, for inviting me," Frick said. "And, good night."

But the marathon nature of the program also has changed. There are now 10 St. Louis Chapter BBWAA Awards given out, as well as 10 speakers to introduce each honoree. The association has whittled things down and the program is usually finished by 10:00 PM. And it always includes a fine dinner, lots of laughs, and lots of baseball vibe.

Fans who attend the dinner receive a commemorative program and stand a decent chance of securing an autograph from one of the honorees, a group that always includes both current and past baseball personalities. If you are lucky enough to secure an invitation, the VIP event preceding the dinner is a chance to get up close and personal with the celebrities in the program.

See a Cards–Cubs Game at Wrigley Field

WHERE: 1060 W. Addison St., Chicago, IL 60613

WHEN: Check the schedule. The Cardinals make three trips a year to Chicago for series with the Cubs.

WHAT TO DO: Get a Cardinals schedule as soon as it comes out, which is usually early September for the following season. Pick out a Cardinals–Cubs weekend in Chicago. Go to www.cubs.com or StubHub and purchase tickets. Go to a travel site and secure a hotel. Start building up a healthy amount of animosity toward the Cubs. A trip to attend a Cardinals–Cubs game should be planned way in advance to ensure availability of tickets and a hotel.

COST: Pricing at Wrigley Field runs from $25 for Upper Reserved Outfield to $280 for Dugout Box. With dynamic pricing, you may be able to find a good deal on StubHub or the Cubs' website at www.cubs.com. The cost of a night or two in a downtown Chicago hotel also has a wide range, depending on the hotel and availability. You're probably looking at somewhere between $150 and $300 a night for the hotel. Toss in cabs, food, and incidentals and it won't be cheap, but it will be memorable.

BUCKET RANK: 🪣🪣🪣🪣🪣

. . . .

If you've watched the Cardinals play the Chicago Cubs on a weekend in St. Louis, or even listened on the radio, you know a ton of fans make the trek from Chicago for the games. In terms of the cheering, the home-field advantage is virtually neutralized. The sea of red is stained with blue.

The same thing happens at Wrigley Field in Chicago. If you haven't been to a weekend day game at the ancient ballpark, you haven't lived as a baseball fan. If you recall, former Cubs manager Lee Elia went on a tirade in 1983 when he called out the "Bleacher Bums" at Wrigley as unemployed drunks who have nothing better to do than come to Wrigley and boo their team.

If that's not enough reason to see a game at Wrigley, I don't know what is.

Part of the experience is staying downtown at the team hotel (the Ritz-Carlton). Not only can you experience the sights and sounds of Chicago's Magnificent Mile, but you might catch a player in the lobby or at the restaurant and snare an autograph.

As far as transportation, you don't want to drive to the ballpark if you can avoid it. Parking is expensive and hard to find. Near Wrigley Field it can be up to $40 or more. If you are willing to walk a ways, you can find something for $20 to $25. Problem is, cars are often boxed in, so if you're planning to leave early, you might be stuck waiting for another driver to arrive. In some places, if you take more than an hour after the game to move your car they will have it towed. Yikes!

Taking a cab is much easier and you will have no problem finding one before the game. They can be a little harder to find outside the ballpark afterward, but if you walk around a bit, you should have no problem flagging one down.

That said, the easiest and cheapest way to get to and from the game is the "L" train. The Red Line stops at Addison Street right outside Wrigley Field and runs straight downtown. For $2.25, you can avoid all the traffic and parking headaches, not to mention enjoy a beer at the game without worrying about transportation. The trains are crowded and sometimes a bit rowdy immediately before and after the games.

If you want to avoid the crowds, and you don't mind walking a little bit, you can take the Brown Line to Southport. There are several good restaurants and watering holes on Southport, but it is about a 15-minute walk to the game. Another option is the bus. The No. 145 and 146 buses run from North Michigan Ave. to Addison and the lakefront. From there, it's a 15-minute stroll to the stadium.

You can experience the game from one of the Wrigleyville Rooftops outside the ballpark, if you can snag some tickets. Wrigleyville Rooftops are available for groups of 1–200 people, with prices ranging from $75 up to $225 for premium games. You would pay a premium price and be hard pressed to find them for a Cardinals–Cubs weekend game.

On the other hand, why would you want to sit outside one of baseball's most historic parks? Inside, you can be part of a major league game played on the same surface, in the same confines, as it was 100 years ago. Only Fenway Park in Boston offers a similar experience.

Certainly, you'll want to arrive in Wrigleyville well before the game to enjoy the environment. Remember, the ballpark is embedded in an actual neighborhood and is surrounded by taverns, restaurants, stores, souvenir shops, and homes. Climb out of a cab, exit the train, and you walk into a world that is buzzing on game day, with people

Yes, it's enemy territory, but Wrigley Field is one of the best away stadiums in which to watch the Cardinals. It's full of history, it's conveniently located in the city limits of Chicago, and you'll be in the company of lots (and lots) of other Cardinals fans. (Jerry Lai–USA TODAY Sports)

and vendors crowding the streets and people heading in every direction around the ballpark.

There are lots of options for eating, drinking, and browsing along Sheffield, Waveland, and Clark avenues. The Cubby Bear or Murphy's Bleachers are well known to Cardinals fans. Goose Island, Lucky's, or McFaddens are also popular choices. Slugger's features batting cages upstairs, if you want to get loose before seeing the first pitch.

The Cardinals–Cubs rivalry is one of the best in sports because of the tone. Because the Cubs have not been to a World Series since 1945, and not won one since 1908, the "rivalry" is mostly good-natured and fan friendly. This is not the Red Sox–Yankees rivalry, where you risk public humiliation and bodily harm in enemy territory.

Go ahead—wear your Cardinals gear, fly the St. Louis flag. You might get some teasing, but there will be plenty of others wearing the Birds on the Bat as well.

WRIGLEY FIELD MOMENTS

There is something special about Wrigley Field for Cubs fans, to be sure. But there also has been something unforgettable about the iconic ballpark if you are a Cardinals fan. As much as the teams and the town, the "Friendly Confines" have played a big part in the entertaining rivalry between the Cardinals and their neighbors that is now more than 120 years old.

If the sun is shining and the wind is blowing, you never know what might happen in a Cardinals–Cubs game at Wrigley. No lead is safe, no deficit insurmountable. Some of the best moments have come in the heat of pennant races—moments connected to Hall of Fame careers, moments a Hall of Fame Player might prefer to erase.

Cardinals Manager Whitey Herzog once said of the unpredictable nature of Wrigley: "I'd be an alcoholic if I had to manage here."

Here are some of the most memorable Wrigley Field games in Cardinals–Cubs history:

July 19–20, 2004

On July 19, in a marquee pitching matchup with Cardinals ace Chris Carpenter, mercurial Cubs right-hander Carlos Zambrano drilled Cardinals center fielder Jim Edmonds with a pitch in the first inning. Edmonds had homered in all three games when the teams met in a three-game series in St. Louis a few days earlier.

In the fourth inning, Edmonds responded by homering again, taking a little extra time to admire the drive, getting under Zambrano's skin. The pitcher screamed at Edmonds as he circled the bases.

Zambrano struck out Edmonds in the sixth inning and for emphasis, wagged his index finger at him as the ball went around the horn. In the eighth, another Cardinals' "MV3," Scott Rolen, clubbed a two-run homer to put the Cardinals ahead 5–3.

The next hitter was Edmonds and, sure enough, Zambrano nailed him again. The two exchanged words and Zambrano was replaced by reliever Mike Remlinger. The Cardinals won the game 5–4. A few days later, Zambrano was suspended for his actions.

On July 20, Japanese outfielder So Taguchi made a spectacular catch in left field and then homered off Kyle Farnsworth to tie the game 8–8 in the eighth inning. The Cardinals then rallied for three in the ninth on homers by Albert Pujols and Reggie Sanders, and won 11–8. His home run was the third of the game for Pujols, who was 5-for-5 with five runs batted in.

September 8–10, 1989

As the series began, the Cubs held a one-and-a-half-game lead over the Cardinals for first place in the National League East standings. In the first game on Friday, the Cardinals trailed 7–1 but rallied for a dramatic 11–8 victory. The big blow was Pedro Guerrero's three-run homer in the eighth off Mitch "Wild Thing" Williams. Guerrero called the blow at the start of the inning, telling teammate Jose DeLeon, "You watch this. If there [are] a couple of men on base when I get up, I'm going deep."

The good times were short-lived for the Cardinals. On Saturday, with a chance to leapfrog the Cubs and jump into first place, the visitors lost 3–2 in extra innings. Journeyman Cubs infielder Luis Salazar tied the game with a two-out single in the eighth, then won it with a double in the 10th. The tying tally was set up when right fielder Tom Brunansky hesitated while relaying the ball back into the infield after Dwight Smith's leadoff single, allowing Smith to take second on the play.

The game took the steam out of the Cardinals. In the series finale the next day, Chicago left-hander Steve Wilson and three relievers combined to strike out 18 Cardinals as the Cubs won 4–1 and moved two-and-a-half games in front.

"You take Friday and the way we lost that game and you don't know if these guys will ever be able to win a game again," Cubs manager Don Zimmer said. "But the way these guys have bounced back is incredible."

The Cubs went on to win a division title, while the Cardinals finished third.

June 23, 1984

In a wild affair many call the greatest Cardinals–Cubs game in history, the Cubs defeated the Cardinals 12–11 in 11 innings. The Cardinals led by as many as six runs in the game—twice! They had leads going into both the bottom of the ninth and 10th innings.

In the ninth, Ryne Sandberg clouted a home run off split-finger ace Bruce Sutter to send the game into extra innings. In the 10th, Sutter and the Cardinals were one strike away from victory when Bob Dernier walked on a 3–2 pitch to bring up Sandberg again. The unthinkable happened—he stepped into another Sutter pitch for another game-tying home run. The Cubs finally won on a single by someone named Dave Owen.

The dramatics spoiled an incredible performance by Willie McGee, who hit for the cycle and drove in six runs for the Cardinals. But the day fell to Sandberg, whose clutch homers were among his five hits and seven RBIs.

Afterward, a shell-shocked Herzog, who had played alongside Mickey Mantle in his career, called Sandberg "the best player I've ever seen."

Cardinals outfielder Andy Van Slyke best summed up the events: "It was like getting knocked down three times in a fight and then KO'ing the guy who knocked you down," Van Slyke said. "And (the Cubs) were knocked down hard."

August 19, 1998

As both chased Roger Maris' single-season home run record, Cubs outfielder Sammy Sosa and Cardinals first baseman Mark McGwire met face to face at Wrigley, tied for the major league lead with 47 homers.

The showdown lived up to the hype, and then some. In the fifth inning, Sosa thrilled the locals and took sole possession of the home run lead by pounding his 48th homer. Fifty-eight minutes later, McGwire answered, clobbering a home run in the eighth inning to tie the game.

In the 10th, "Big Mac" did it again, hitting his 49th homer to send the Cardinals to an 8–6 victory and regain the upper hand in the home run derby.

McGwire would go on to hit 70 home runs, a record that lasted only three seasons, while Sosa also surpassed Maris and finished with 66. For McGwire, the drama that took place at Wrigley that day was especially enjoyable.

"I've never been associated with a major league team where there was so much excitement between two teams," he said after the game.

May 13, 1958

"Swing, and there it is..." Those were the excited words of Harry Caray as he described Stan "the Man" Musial's 3,000th hit in front of a tiny crowd of less than 6,000 on a Tuesday afternoon at Wrigley.

Wanting Musial to get his historic blow at home, Cardinals manager Fred Hutchinson held No. 6 out of the starting lineup. But he couldn't resist using Musial to pinch-hit for pitcher Sam Jones in the sixth inning. The 37-year-old Musial doubled off Moe Drabowsky, chasing home Gene Green and igniting a four-run rally.

At the time, Musial was only the eighth player in history to reach the 3,000 mark, the first since Paul Waner in 1942. The Cardinals won 5–3.

That night, the team headed back to St. Louis. When the train pulled to a stop in Clinton, Illinois, a crowd was standing on the station platform chanting, "We want Musial!" Musial came out, shook hands, and signed autographs. Farther down the track, in Springfield, Illinois, an even larger crowd was gathered, calling Musial's name and singing "For He's a Jolly Good Fellow."

Again, Musial accommodated by greeting the fans and signing autographs. Finally, the train pulled into Union Station, where more than 1,000 fans were waiting. Musial was led to a platform where he thanked the crowd and told them, "Now, I know how Charles Lindbergh felt."

The next night, with a crowd of more than 20,000 at old Busch Stadium, the incomparable Musial gave them a proper thank you, homering in his first at-bat.

"When I think about all those people coming out to the train station, it's just really incredible," Musial said years later. "I mean, can you imagine something like that today? The fans really were great to me."

September 7–9, 1973

Manager Red Schoendienst's Cardinals led the NL East with a 72–68 record, with the Mets, Pirates, Cubs, and Expos in hot pursuit. The Cubs won the first game of the series 8–2 behind Burt Hooton. Pete LaCock's pinch, two-run double was the key blow in a six-run sixth for the Cubs.

The North Siders also won the second game as Don Kessinger snapped a 1–1 tie with a run-scoring single in the seventh and Ron Santo homered for insurance in the eighth. The Cubs then made a clean sweep of things in the third game, with Billy Williams launching an eighth-inning homer off Al Hrabosky that keyed the 5–4 victory.

The series touched off a seven-game losing streak for the Cardinals, a skid from which they never recovered. They finished second with an 81–81 record, one-and-a-half games behind the New York Mets. The Cubs wound up fifth, five games back.

The Cardinals and Cubs shared 124 seasons of baseball and 2,363 regular-season games before they finally met in a postseason. The I-70 Series between the Cardinals and the Kansas City Royals was unique in 1985, but this was epic.

And frankly, for the Cardinals, it just didn't get any better. No, really, it did not get better—they lost to Joe Maddon's North Siders in four.

Despite the Cards' 100–62 regular-season record, that was not especially surprising. There was a sense the club was in trouble as the playoffs began. The pitching was disheveled, the lineup was unstable, the production was thin, and the season ended with six losses over nine games. Dead team walking.

The Cardinals won Game 1 of the series at home behind Lackey. But Jaime Garcia's bizarre, upset-tummy start sent things tumbling in a different direction. The Cubs won Game 2, then hit nine home runs over the next 18 innings to slam the Cardinals.

You know what they say: If you can't beat 'em, sign a big fat contract and join 'em. When it was all said and done, Lackey and Heyward did just that, taking free-agent deals to sleep with the enemy.

The bleachers at Wrigley are completely separate from the rest of the stadium. That is, you can only enter at the back of the structure and there is no access to the rest of the stadium. The bleachers feature open seating and to sit near the field, you'd best get there at least an hour ahead of time.

The rest of the stadium has only three other entrances. The stadium club entrance on Addison is usually faster when the park opens and is available to anyone. When the game is over, leaving the ballpark is slow, so you might want to position yourself near an exit once the final outs are in sight.

The food at Wrigley is not the best, so you'd be wise to bring a sandwich or something to snack on. The beer choices are mundane—mostly Budweiser products—but there are a select few stands that sell a better variety. The best place to get a beer might be the Dunkin Donuts concession by the front entrance—not many people realize it sells beer.

Beer sales stop at the end of the eighth inning, so don't let that seventh-inning stretch go to waste. Weather can be, and often is, an issue. It usually is cold early in the season. Wrigley is less than a mile from Lake Michigan, so in the spring it goes from sunny to cloudy, and from 60 degrees to 40 degrees, in no time. On a cool day, a good seating choice is the upper deck above the main entrance. It is in the sun, can provide some warmth, has beer nearby, and features a beautiful view of the city.

On a bright, sunny day, be sure to bring sunscreen, especially if you are sitting in the bleachers.

Down two games to none to the Boston Red Sox, the Cardinals trailed 1–0 in the third inning of Game 3 at Busch Stadium when they got something going. Suppan singled, Edgar Renteria doubled, and runners were at second and third with nobody out. Slugging Larry Walker stepped to the plate; Albert Pujols was on deck.

Admit it; this was running through your head at the time: "The Cardinal will cash in here. They will go on to win Game 3. The series will be 2–1. The worm has turned." If you're a Cardinals fan, you couldn't help but think that way.

The Red Sox played the infield back, hoping to avoid the big inning, so when Walker grounded to second, it was an automatic run. Or was it?

After starting down the line, Suppan inexplicably stopped between third and home and tried to retreat. He was caught in no man's land. Stunned first baseman David Ortiz fired to third and Suppan was tagged out, turning Walker's grounder into a double play. Pujols grounded out and the inning was over. Boston went on to win 4–1, then finished the Cardinals for a World Series sweep in Game 4.

It being the World Series, Suppan's pratfall got national attention. Some have called it the worst base-running play in World Series history. That seems overstated, given Babe Ruth got thrown out trying to steal second to end Game 7 of the 1926 World Series.

Was it a bad play? No question. But let's be fair here. Suppan did not earn his keep on the base paths. He had a total of four hits during the regular season and scored just three runs. Expecting him to be a savvy base runner is like expecting Rush Limbaugh to be speechless.

Years later, Suppan makes no excuses. He'll grant you that play was a nail in the coffin, but just one of the nails.

"In a championship series, each game is like a series in itself," Suppan said. "In that game, that was a huge mistake. But I don't think everyone quit at that point, because we didn't get that run. Did it change momentum? Yeah, it might have. I wish it hadn't happened, but it did."

That said, to hold Suppan accountable, to suggest that mistake was *the* reason the Cardinals were overwhelmed by the Red-hot Sox, is plain silly.

Consider some context: the 2004 Cardinals might have been the best everyday lineup the team has ever put on the field. Ever.

"The real shame of it is, if we could have kept it going and won that World Series, that team would be considered one of the greatest baseball teams ever to play, I think," said current Cardinals manager Mike Matheny, the hard-nosed receiver of that team. "It was that good, the best team I ever played on."

Postseason and regular season combined, the '04 Cardinals won 112 games, more than any team in the history of a franchise that is more than 120 seasons old. It was the first Cardinals team to win as many as 105 regular season games in 60 years, or since the 1944 world champions won as many.

The '04 Cardinals didn't just win a division title—they slam-dunked it, finishing 13 games ahead of the runner-up Astros. The lead was in double figures on July 21, just 94 games into the summer.

In that remarkable season, the Cardinals averaged 5.3 runs per game. They scored five runs or more in 92 of their 162 starts. They hit 214 home runs and led the National League in hits (1,544), runs (855), RBIs (817), batting average (.278), and slugging percentage (.460).

Meanwhile, their pitching staff finished second in the league with a 3.75 ERA and led the league in saves (57). Oh, and there's much, much more.

On the defense, the 2004 squad had three Gold Glove winners in Matheny, center fielder Jim Edmonds, and third baseman Scott Rolen.

Two other defenders—shortstop Edgar Renteria and first baseman Albert Pujols—were Gold Gloves at other times in their careers. So that's five GG-caliber players in the field.

Then there were the "MV3s." In the middle of it all, the lineup was centered around Pujols, Rolen, and Edmonds. Individually, they each had at least 34 homers and at least 111 runs. Combined, they collected 122 home runs, 121 doubles, 344 runs, 358 RBIs, and 24.8 Wins Above Replacement.

They finished third (Pujols), fourth (Rolen), and fifth (Edmonds) in the voting for the National League MVP Award.

Now, on to the heart of the matter, or why that team was swept in the World Series by Boston.

Those same MV3s—Pujols, Edmonds, and Rolen—went a combined 6-for-45 with no home runs and 1 RBI in the four games. Over the final 28 innings of the '04 World Series, the Cardinals' offense generated 14 hits in 100 at-bats (.140) and three runs.

In all, the Deadbirds struck out 32 times and batted .190 over the four games; in short, one base-running blunder does not a World Series meltdown make. Over the last seven postseason games they played, the Red Sox did not trail for 60 consecutive innings. That's not incidental; that's what is known as trending.

In contrast, the Red Sox clipped Cardinals pitching for 39 hits, 24 walks, and 24 runs in 34 innings. The runaway Red Sox train overcame a 3–0 deficit to beat the Yankees in the ALCS.

This was not a bad base-running issue; this was a total eclipse.

So appreciate Jeff "Soup" Suppan for the thrills he helped provide, and the delightful sports grill he owns in the Los Angeles area. The 2004 World Series failure was not his fault.

as is a signed guitar from Tom Petty. Not to worry, it's anchored to the wall, not "free-falling."

There is even a picture of the St. Louis beat writers from Suppan's time in St. Louis on the stairway leading up to the rooftop patio. Or is it that stairway leading down? Hmmm?

If you get the urge, and can find a catcher, a pitching mound is available on the patio. And if you're lucky, Suppan might be wearing his 2006 World Series championship ring, which he will happily show and tell.

Family patriarch and veteran chef Larry Suppan makes the exquisite desserts, which include Boston cream pie, apple brittle and ice cream, and cheesecake. Jeff's brother Dan pitches in—sorry, pun intended—with plenty of business advice.

The cheesesteak sandwich is the top-selling item, but the sliders with beer-battered fries ain't a bad way to go either.

Suppan keeps his line in the baseball waters. He is a scout for Kansas City Royals and helps out with the Crespi High baseball team when he can. He pitched five years for the Royals before he arrived in St. Louis. With both cities fielding contending teams, he is sometimes asked by patrons to pick sides.

But Suppan was highly respected during his playing career for his ability to walk the line of neutrality, his innate talent of saying something without ever saying anything.

"I root for the restaurant," Suppan tells those wanting him to choose sides "I root for Soup's Sports Grill."

Fair enough.

Eat at Harry Caray's Restaurant

WHERE: 33 West Kinzie Street, Chicago, IL 60654

WHEN: Anytime you're in Chicago. Normal hours are 11:30 AM to 10:30 PM. Friday–Saturday it stays open until 11:00 PM. On Sunday, the hours are 3:00 PM to 10:00 PM.

WHAT TO DO: Walk, drive, grab a cab, or hop on the train to Harray Caray's Italian Steakhouse. If making dinner plans, call 312-828-0966, or visit www.harrycarays.com to make reservations.

COST: Likely in the $30–$50 range per person, more if you're having a steak. A bone-in rib eye is $52.95.

BUCKET RANK:

arry Christopher Carabina—his real name—became an icon in Chicago after broadcasting White Sox games for 11 years, then Cubs games for his final 16 years. But truth be told, he belonged to St. Louis first.

Caray was born and raised in St. Louis, played semipro baseball as a youth, and was hired as an announcer for the Cardinals in 1945. He also broadcast St. Louis Hawks NBA games, St. Louis Flyers AHL games, and University of Missouri football, and even did a couple of seasons of the American League St. Louis Browns games (1945–46).

Caray was the radio voice of the Cardinals through three pennants and three World Series appearances in 1964, 1967, and 1968. He famously called Stan Musial's 3,000[th] hit on May 13, 1958, which coincidentally happened at Wrigley Field in Chicago, as well as Bob

Gibson's remarkable 17-strikeout performance in Game 1 of the 1968 World Series.

During his time in St. Louis, Caray became especially adept at selling "ice-cold Busch Bavarian," and calling home runs as follows:"There it goes...it might be...it could be...it is!" And he was merciless on players like third baseman Ken Boyer, with calls like "ground ball...right though Boyer's legs...boy, oh boy."

Caray was also rumored to have played a part in getting General Manger Bing Devine fired during the 1964 season, and he was rumored to have had an affair with August Busch III's wife, Susan. Both Caray and the former Mrs. Busch denied any hanky-panky ever took place.

In November 1968, Caray was nearly killed when he was hit by a car late at night on Kingshighway. A car driven by Michael Poliquin, 21, a Vietnam War veteran from Overland, Missouri, struck Caray as he crossed the street to enter the Chase Park Plaza Hotel. A *Sporting News* account at the time reported Caray "was knocked 40 feet in the air. His shoes were found 25 feet south of the hotel and he landed 40 feet north." He suffered compound fractures in both legs, a broken right shoulder, a broken nose, and facial cuts.

Cardinals owner "Gussie" Busch gave Caray the use of his Florida home while he recovered from his injuries. At the same time, according to some reports, Busch was having the FBI look into the rumors about the announcer and his wife. What's the expression: keep your friends close, and your enemies even closer?

With little fanfare, after 25 years of doing Cardinals games, the popular Caray was canned after the 1969 season. Soon after, Gussie and Susan Busch were divorced. You do the math.

Caray went to Oakland in 1970, lasing one season with controversial A's owner Charley Finely. Reportedly, Finley wanted Caray to change his famous "Holy Cow!" call to "Holy Mule!"

In 1971, Caray wound up in Chicago as the play-by-play man for the White Sox, becoming hugely popular on the South Side, along with partner Jimmy Piersall. Caray would occasionally broadcast day games while sitting bare-chested in the bleachers. He also started his practice of leading the crowd in singing "Take Me Out to the Ball Game" during the seventh-inning stretch.

Caray moved to the North Side after the 1981 season, and his timing was excellent. The perennial also-ran Cubs won a rare division title in 1984 and, working for cable television superstation WGN, Caray became nationally renowned.

Harry Caray's Italian Steakhouse in Chicago's River North neighborhood opened in 1987, and Caray was a regular there after Cubs games until his death in 1998. The restaurant itself is worth seeing, housed in an architectural landmark building once home to infamous mob enforcer Frank Nitti. You can see relics from those gangster days in Frank Nitti's Vault, which includes a once-hidden underground tunnel.

The Harry Caray restaurant group now has additional locations in Rosemont and Lombard. Adjacent to Harry Caray's Lombard is Holy Mackerel!, the group's fresh-seafood concept. Harry Caray's Tavern Navy Pier has a family-friendly menu and spectacular waterfront location. Harry Caray's 7th Inning Stretch and the Chicago Sports Museum anchor the seventh floor of Water Tower Place and combine to create a 23,000-square-foot complex offering dining, entertainment, private event venues, and retail. There's even a Harry Caray's at Midway Airport for those just passing through.

But the downtown restaurant is the original article, one of the city's top dining spots and a must-stop for visiting Cardinals fans. The restaurant was named the "Best Italian Steakhouse" by a *Chicago Tribune* Dining Poll, according to the restaurant website.

There is a lunch and a dinner menu, each containing a wide variety of options, a formal dining area with a warm ambience, and a sports bar with a number of televisions. The menu features burgers, pasta, steaks, salads, sandwiches, gluten-free meals, beer, wine, and a variety of cocktails.

Harry Caray's is also known for a large baseball-memorabilia collection, featuring lots of pictures and newspaper clippings. You can see everything from Caray's famous oversized glasses to the "Bartman Ball"—or remnants of the ball Steve Bartman infamously snared during Game 6 of the 2003 National League Championship Series.

And while you're there, be sure to have a picture taken with the bust of Harry Caray, as have Barack Obama, Cameron Diaz, Ben Roethlisberger, Ben Stein, Dennis Rodman, George Foreman, Dog the Bounty Hunter…and just about everyone else who has stopped in.

Holy Mule!

Eat at
Mike Shannon's Grill

WHERE: 871 S. Arbor Vitae, Suite 101, Edwardsville, IL 62025 or 10701 Lambert International Boulevard, St. Louis, MO 63145

WHEN: Times vary, so call to make sure.

WHAT TO DO: Make reservations at Mike Shannon's Steaks and Seafood at mikeshannonsgrill.com or stop by the airport location on your next trip in or out of town.

COST: Shannon's is a little pricey, but well worth the experience. Dinner for two will probably run in the $150–$200 range. I recommend the bone-in filet.

BUCKET RANK: 🪣🪣🪣

What a lot of people probably don't know about Cardinals radio announcer Mike Shannon is that he is arguably the greatest athlete ever to come out of the St. Louis area. When he was a senior at CBC High School in St. Louis in 1957, he was named the Missouri High School Player of the Year in both basketball and football. He remains the only local high school athlete ever to be honored with both awards in the same year.

He attended the University of Missouri in 1957–58 as a promising young college quarterback. Shannon is quick to tell people he would have stayed with football if there had been more money in it at the time, because he considered himself a much better football player than baseball player.

The Missouri football coach at the time, Frank Broyles, commented that, had he stayed in school, Shannon might have won the Heisman Trophy as the best college player in the country. Instead, Shannon left Missouri in 1958 and signed a contract with the Cardinals. He has been a part of the organization ever since.

Shannon was called up to the big leagues in 1962 and played on Cardinals teams that won three pennants and two world championships from 1964 through 1968. Shannon came up through the minors as a strong-armed outfielder. In 1966, he was first in the National League in fielding percentage (.992) for right fielders and turned four double plays from the outfield. But in 1967, when the club needed to make room for newly acquired right fielder Roger Maris, Shannon moved to third base.

The versatile athlete even donned the "tools of ignorance" and appeared in five games as a catcher during the 1965 and 1966 seasons. Over nine big-league seasons, Shannon had 68 home runs, 367 runs batted in, and a .255 average. In 1968, the "Year of the Pitcher," he finished seventh in the National League MVP voting by batting .266 with 15 homers and 79 RBIs.

Shannon hit a home run in each of the three World Series he played in. He is also the answer to stadium trivia, having hit the last

Cardinals home run at the original Busch Stadium (aka Sportsman's Park) and the first Cardinals home run when the team moved into Busch Stadium II.

But Shannon's playing career came to an abrupt end in 1970 when it was discovered he had nephritis, a kidney disease.

"I remember when we found out, I wasn't worried about myself," he said. "But I was worried about my wife and my five kids—how they were going to be if I didn't make it."

Shannon attempted to come back from the setback, but…"I slid into second base one day, and the doctor said, 'OK, that's it. You're done.' A year or two later, (General Manager) Bing Devine was willing to give me another chance to come back, but I looked at the team they had then and said, "Nah, I don't think so. I'd just screw the whole team up."

That's when Shannon's second Cardinals career began. After spending a year in the team's promotional office, Shannon moved to the broadcast booth and became the color-analyst sidekick to Hall of Fame broadcaster Jack Buck.

Following Buck's death in 2002, Shannon took over the lead role and has been at it ever since, though in 2016 he announced he would no longer broadcast road games for the club. In 2014 he was elected into the Cardinals Hall of Fame in a ceremony at Ballpark Village. Going back to his first season in 1958, with the Cardinals' Class D Albany affiliate in the Georgia-Florida League, Shannon has had birds on his bat in some capacity for 58 years.

As a player, Shannon became known to his teammates as "Moon Man." Hall of Fame pitcher Bob Gibson once explained: "He'll talk 15 minutes and when he's through you'll go away scratching your head and wondering what he said," Gibson said. "He may start a conversation about baseball and end up with insurance after going through 45 other topics. You still don't know what he said."

The nickname stuck and so did the interesting monologues. Those same "Shannonisms" are part of what has endeared him to Cardinals radio audiences all these years. No one will forget the night the Cardinals were playing under a full moon in New York, when No. 18 looked to the sky and said, "I wish you folks back in St. Louis could see this moon."

No doubt, if you love the Cardinals, you love Shannon and you have to experience his restaurants. Mike Shannon's Steaks and Seafood, formerly at 620 Market Street in St. Louis, two blocks north of the ballpark, was a St. Louis institution. It offered fine dining in a warm, elegant atmosphere, with more than 500 photos and a great collection of baseball memorabilia.

If you never got to experience Shannon's downtown location before it closed in January 2016, don't fret. In March 2013 the owners opened Mike Shannon's Grill at 871 S. Arbor Vitae, Suite JOJ, in nearby Edwardsville, Illinois. And in 2014 the powers-that-be added a third sister location inside Lambert-St. Louis International Airport, across from Gate A12. The airport location has some 90 seats in the dining and bar areas, featuring dark leather upholstery accented by wood finishes and complemented with a display of baseballs, bats, jerseys, and sports memorabilia.

Chapter 5

Things to See

Experience Opening Day in St. Louis

WHERE: St. Louis, MO, and the immediate surrounding area

WHEN: The day the Cardinals play their first home game of a new season. The ballpark gates open two hours before the actual game, but there are rallies, pregame festivities...lots going on before the first pitch.

WHAT TO DO: Buy a ticket and enjoy the show, but don't procrastinate. Tickets go fast. The Cardinals had a record sellout of 47,875 for their home opener in 2015. Be downtown early and enjoy all the related activities.

COST: With "Dynamic Pricing," you can normally buy a reserved ticket to a Cardinals game for as little as $18 and as much as $500 for the Commissioner's Box. There are parking lots around the ballpark, ranging from $10 to $30, depending on location.

BUCKET RANK:

. . . .

Mark Reynolds had spent eight seasons in the big leagues, in places like Baltimore, New York, Milwaukee, and Arizona. But he had never entered a ballpark quite like he did on April 13, 2015, the home opener at Busch Stadium III.

Reynolds arrived on the field riding in the bed of a new pickup truck. He hopped out to shake hands with Red Schoendienst, Bob Gibson, Lou Brock, Ozzie Smith, Bruce Sutter, Whitey Herzog, Tony La Russa, Willie McGee, Jim Edmonds, and Mike Shannon, then made his way over to the first-base line to stand alongside his teammates.

"I've never seen anything like it," Reynolds said. "I mean, you're riding in the car, the horses, the (American) eagle, shaking hands with Hall of Famers...what a spectacle."

Let's face it, Opening Day is special in every Major League Baseball town in America. The return of the national pastime is an annual rite of spring: the promise of sunnier days ahead, the opportunity to dream before the sometimes-stark reality of the regular season sets in.

But Opening Day in St. Louis is more than that. It's what Jim Nantz would call "a tradition unlike any other." It's a celebration of the past and the present; it's an identity the city and players embrace wholeheartedly.

"Everybody has their own traditions for Opening Day," manager Mike Matheny says, "but it just seems like it's a little bigger here and a little deeper. I allow myself to watch the Clydesdales and the Hall of Famers come through. How many people get to ride around in front of 40,000 and have them cheer?"

Opening Day is an official unofficial holiday in St. Louis. If you don't show for school, work, or any other type of appointment, no explanation is needed. Downtown is buzzing with traffic in the streets and on the sidewalks, and the setting around the ballpark is spectacular.

Located immediately adjacent to the stadium, Ballpark Village comes alive with bands playing, rallies blaring, and a "sea of red" fans everywhere. Inside Busch Stadium, the festivities usually begin some 45 minutes before game time.

The show starts when the wagon gates open and the Budweiser Clydesdales appear, pulling a wagon full of the choicest products of the brewer operating 12 blocks away. The eight-horse hitch, along with two drivers and a Dalmatian, circle the stadium to the Budweiser theme, "Here Comes the King."

At this point, the song has no direct connection to the team. The sponsored stadium name notwithstanding, Anheuser-Busch sold the

Cardinals to the group of investors led by Bill DeWitt Jr. in December 1995. But over the years, the prohibition jingle has become much more than beer-swilling encouragement.

Following the Clydesdales, local dignitaries are introduced, such as the governor, the mayor, and the county executive. Appropriately enough, some might say, team mascot Fredbird is introduced to the crowd next, joined by Team Fredbird, his support group of young cheerleaders.

Next a motorcade of National Baseball Hall of Fame and Museum members arrives. Riding in red convertibles, each of the organization's living members enters the stadium and circles the warning track, waving to the crowd. In 2015, that parade was followed by a clip on the video board highlighting great players and moments from the past to the present.

Then, members of the Cardinals Hall of Fame Museum in Ballpark Village step from the dugout and join members of the Cooperstown club around home plate. Then the gates open again and the current Cardinals circle the field in another motorcade, each riding in the back of a red pickup truck.

One by one, the current players hop out at home plate and make the rounds, shaking the hands of each of the various Hall of Fame Players before taking their place along the first-base line. The opposing team is also introduced and lines up in front of its dugout along the third-base line.

At that point, a color guard presents the United States flag in center field, with servicemen and women from nearby Ft. Leonard Wood handling the detail. Then an American bald eagle swoops through the stadium, making several loops before returning to a trainer's arm.

In 2015, the moments included a video tribute to young outfielder Oscar Taveras, who was killed in car accident in the Dominican Republic after the 2014 season ended.

The national anthem is performed before the ceremonial first pitch is thrown. In 2015, popular former outfielder Willie McGee did the honors, with Hall of Fame shortstop Ozzie Smith doing the catching.

That's followed by the proclamation everyone is waiting for: "Play Ball!"

See a Game at AutoZone Park in Memphis

WHERE: 200 Union Avenue, Memphis, TN 38103

WHEN: 72 home dates to choose from, between April and September

WHAT TO DO: Pick a game or two from the Redbirds' schedule, available on the team's website at www.memphisredbirds.com. Make the trip to Memphis, which is a 280-mile drive south on I-55 from St. Louis. Stay at the Doubletree Hotel across the street from AutoZone Park. See the Cardinals' Class AAA affiliate play and scout players you might see, or have seen, in St. Louis.

COST: All depends on where you're coming from. Major airlines fly to Memphis, including American, Delta, and United. Airfare, at least from St. Louis, is in the $400–$500 neighborhood. An individual ticket to a Redbirds game runs from $6 to $55. A night at the Doubletree will be around $170, if booked in advance. With great barbecue, Beale Street, and other attractions nearby, the food and beverage cost could run high—depending on willpower.

BUCKET RANK: 🪣🪣

For a Cardinals fan living in St. Louis, the 280-mile drive down I-55 South is well worth the effort. If you are a Cardinals fan living elsewhere, it's still a must-do trip. For one thing, it's Memphis, home of the blues, of Beale Street, of famous barbecue, of Graceland, for God's sake.

For another, it's the Memphis Redbirds, where the legend of Stubby Clapp was born.

The Canadian-born Clapp never made much of a splash in the major leagues. In 2001, he played in 23 games for the Cardinals, getting five hits in 25 at-bats and one run batted in. But at Class Memphis, where he played four seasons (1999–2002), he was the most popular player in franchise history. Like Ozzie Smith in St. Louis, Clapp used to do a backflip as he took his infield position, capturing the attention of the crowd.

A 5'8" overachiever, Clapp's hard work and enthusiasm struck a chord with a city that embraced the same values. He was often referred to as the "Mayor of Memphis." During the 2002 season, he was featured on a growth chart for kids, sponsored by a Memphis-area medical group. In 2009, he was named one of the Memphis area's "Athletes of the Decade."

On April 21, 2007, Clapp's No. 10 Memphis jersey became the first number ever retired by the Memphis Redbirds. The distinction is commemorated by a painted "10" on the wall above the Redbirds' bullpen at AutoZone Park.

And, as if that's not enough, three years later the club held "Ode to Clapping Night," which included giveaways of a Stubby Clapp bobblehead doll.

Eat your heart out, Elvis.

Even if you're not there specifically to honor Sir Clapp, you will have a blast attending a game at AutoZone Park. The Memphis Redbirds joined the Pacific Coast League (PCL) as an expansion team in 1998. They were owned as a nonprofit community entity until being acquired by the Cardinals organization in November 2013, a purchase completed in 2014.

The Redbirds have made it to the PCL playoffs on four occasions and have won league championships in 2000 and 2009. But it doesn't seem like anyone in Memphis is really counting. They just enjoy baseball and enjoy their dynamic ballpark, which opened in 2000 and has maintained a state-of-the-art feel.

From the recently added video board—3,600 square feet of HD love— to the veggie hot dogs and BBQ nachos, a trip to this enchanting yard is one of the best experiences in baseball, at any level.

The stadium, which replaced Tim McCarver Stadium as the home of the Redbirds, is located in the middle of downtown Memphis and is surrounded by other attractions. If you can't stay at the Doubletree, a number of attractive alternatives fit the bill, including the famous Peabody Hotel, also within walking distance of the ballpark.

AutoZone made a point to borrow elements from ballparks like Camden Yards, Wrigley Field, and Fenway Park in its design. The outfield walls measure 319 feet down the left-field line, 400 feet to center, and 322 feet down the right-field line. The power alleys are 360 feet in left, 373 feet in right—which makes left-handed-swinging Rick Ankiel's 32 home runs for Memphis in 2007 all the more impressive. There are about 8,000 seats and standing room brings capacity to 10,000.

The atmosphere for a Redbirds game is not unlike the atmosphere at Busch Stadium. The amenities of the ballpark tend to neutralize the intensity level and keep crowds entertained, whether the home team does or not. The fans are definitely into it when the Redbirds are winning, but they're not devastated otherwise. It is a fun, family environment.

Keep in mind, this is Memphis. When a night game is over, there is plenty more entertainment where that came from, though geared more toward adults. Beale Street is blocks away, where blues legends like W.C. Handy and B.B. King got their start. Both have clubs that rock well into the morning, along with a number of other bars and restaurants on the strip.

If you care to expand your reconnaissance to downtown, you can enjoy the barbecue from Rendezvous or Central, or maybe some fried chicken at Gus's.

Otherwise, if you have the time and the transportation, you could drive 14 minutes down I-240 and visit Graceland.

Of course, once you've had a chance to see Stubby Clapp's retired number, what would be the point?

See Cardinals Exhibits at the National Baseball Hall of Fame and Museum in Cooperstown

WHERE: 25 Main Street, Cooperstown, NY 13326

WHEN: The museum is open from 9:00 AM to 9:00 PM

WHAT TO DO: The big trick is how to get there. Cooperstown is located in a rather remote area of the state. For instance, the town is about 1,000 miles from St. Louis and at least 30 miles or so from any interstate highway. Flights are available to the following large airports, each approximately 90 miles away: Albany International Airport in Albany, New York; Syracuse Hancock International Airport in Syracuse, New York; and Greater Binghamton Airport in Binghamton, New York.

Depending on your mode of travel, the best bet is to fly in to Albany, rent a car, and make the 72-mile drive to Cooperstown.

COST: Your travel costs aside, admission to the museum is $23 for adults, $15 for seniors (65 and over), $12 for children (ages 7 through 12), and $12 for veterans. Children (6 and under) and active military members are admitted free. There is special pricing for group visits.

BUCKET RANK: 🪣🪣🪣🪣

This item should be on the bucket list of any fan, regardless of team or player most admired. The Cardinals are no exception, with a number of special exhibits and memories presented for viewing at the Hall of Fame.

As mentioned, getting to the Hall can be a haul. Then again, maybe that's how it should be. The museum is located in a tiny, 1,852-person Otsego County village, some three-and-a-half hours from New York City—and that's by design.

Most historians these days will tell you that Abner Doubleday did not truly invent the game of baseball in Cooperstown in 1939. But, genuine or not, the story certainly is part of baseball lore and Doubleday, a Union general in the Civil War, once lived in the Cooperstown area.

During the Great Depression, Cooperstown and other surrounding towns were in desperate need of money and advancing the legend of Doubleday was one way to make a buck. If St. Andrews, Scotland, can be the birthplace of golf, why not make Cooperstown the birthplace of baseball? At least, that's the way Hall of Fame founder Stephen Carlton Clark saw it. And the rest is history, literally and figuratively.

The first Hall of Fame class of 1936 featured Ty Cobb, Babe Ruth, Honus Wagner, Christy Mathewson, and Walter Johnson as its inductees. Let's face it: with a few individual exceptions, just about every election since has been a compromise.

Cooperstown is a sleepy, one-stoplight town that comes to life one week each July for the induction of a new class. There were no Cardinals in that original class, but there have been 17 players and mangers inducted into the Hall of Fame since who list the Cardinals as their primary team. The most recent Cardinal alumnus honored was manager Tony La Russa. In the same class was another great Cardinal, Joe Torre, who played six years in St. Louis and was voted the National League MVP as a Cardinal in 1971, when he led the league in batting (.363), runs batted in (137), hits (230), and total bases (352).

However, Torre was admitted to the Hall of Fame as a manager. He managed the Cardinals for six seasons, but his HOF apprenticeship took place in New York, where he skippered the Pinstripes to four World Series wins and six pennants. You can see artifacts from Torre's career with both the Cardinals and the Yankees.

The three block strip of Main Street in Cooperstown is as baseball touristy as it comes. It is packed with souvenir and memorabilia shops and sprinkled with restaurants, all featuring the baseball theme. The museum itself, located at the far end of town, is much more unassuming. The red-brick building doesn't look much different from any other city library or government building.

The view inside is considerably different. It's much bigger than it appears on the outside, packed with precious artifacts and memories of the national pastime, its biggest names and biggest moments. The Hall of Fame offers more than 40,000 three-dimensional exhibits, as well as innumerable plaques, mounted presentations, books, and baseball cards. Keep in mind that at any given time, only 15 percent of the museum's collection is on display.

What's more, the place can be crowded on a summer day, even if it's not induction week. With nearly every step, there is so much to see and experience, you would be cheating yourself by trying to do it all in just one day.

The senior curator at the National Baseball Hall of Fame and Museum, St. Louis native Tom Shieber, agreed. "If you're a Cardinal fan, you probably like baseball in general," he said. "And if you're a baseball fan, you need to spend more than a day."

But of course, this a bucket list for Cardinals fans, so let's cut to the chase and identify some must-see exhibits for that demographic. And make no mistake: there is no lack of Redbird representation here. Cardinals-related material touches on the careers of Rogers Hornsby, Red Schoendienst, Bob Gibson, Lou Brock, Dizzy Dean, Ozzie Smith, and Bruce Sutter, just to name a few.

If you had to narrow it down to one must-see Cardinals exhibit, it probably would be Stan "the Man" Musial's locker from old Sportsman's Park. Musial's No. 6 jersey is hanging, along with his stirrup socks. A cap and a ball sit on the stool and nearby is the lineup card from his final game on September 29, 1963.

A few of the other Cardinals-related things to see:

- MVP medal awarded to Cardinals second baseman Rogers Hornsby after he won the second of his Triple Crowns in 1925

- The tattered remains of David Freese's Cardinals jersey, torn by the celebrating teammates that greeted him after his walk-off home run won Game 6 of the 2011 World Series

- Dizzy Dean's 1934 jersey, the year he was 30–7 and was named the National League's Most Valuable Player. There has not been a pitcher win as many as 30 games in the NL since.

- The Carl Yastrzemski–model glove worn by Bob Gibson in 1968, when he had a 1.12 earned run average and 13 shutouts. There's nothing there to explain how Gibson (22–9) lost nine games that season.

- An oversized pair of eyeglasses worn by Harry Caray. The specs became his signature look as the longtime announcer for the Chicago Cubs, but way before that, Harry was the play-by-play voice of the Cardinals from 1945 through 1969.

- The trademark Stetson hat worn by Dean when he began doing the "Game of the Week" on TV in 1953

- Mark McGwire's bat from September 27, 1998, when he hit his 69th and 70th home runs of the season

Cardinals fans will also want to make a stop in the media section of the museum, where they'll find the likes of *St. Louis Post-Dispatch* beat writers Rick Hummel, Bob Broeg, and J. Roy Stockton honored. You can also see exhibits honoring both Cary and the beloved Jack Buck, who handled the play-by-play for Cardinals audiences for 47 years.

Speaking at the 1987 induction ceremonies in Cooperstown, Buck said, "I don't want to be belligerent about it but I kind of think, Mr. (George) Steinbrenner and others, that St. Louis is, not only the heartland of America, but the best baseball city in the United States."

If you prefer to visit Cooperstown during a Hall of Fame induction week, you better book early. There are a few hotel choices and a number of quaint bed-and-breakfast options but remember, we're talking about a small town. Check the accommodations in Cooperstown first, then work your way out to surrounding towns or back toward the interstates. Expect prices for induction week to be much higher than normal.

The Cooperstown area offers a variety of lodging and dining options, from a quaint bed-and-breakfast to a full-service luxury resort, from fine dining to sports bars. You can stay in Cooperstown, in one of the surrounding villages, or in the more-urban setting of Oneonta. Go to www.cooperstowngetaway.org, www.cooperstownchamber.org, or www.thisiscooperstown.com for more help.

Shieber suggests the best time to visit the Hall of Fame might be late fall or winter, when crowds are nonexistent and the prices are friendly.

"It's 24/7 baseball," Shieber explained. "But there are minimum crowds at that time of year. You can watch the postseason games on TV and the trees make it prime leaf-peeping season."

In other words, to borrow from one of Buck's signature phrases, if you're talking about a Hall of Fame visit, "That's a winter."

Watch The Pride of St. Louis

Cardinals great Pepper Martin once said of his teammate, Dizzy Dean, "When Ol' Diz was out there pitching it was more than just another ballgame. It was a regular three-ring circus and everybody was wide awake and enjoying being alive."

There have been a lot of memorable ballplayers, a lot of Hall of Fame Players, but there have been few personalities more colorful in the game than Jay Hanna Dean. He was the Muhammad Ali of baseball at a time—the Great Depression—when the game desperately needed one.

Dean's career was relatively short, sabotaged by a freak injury he suffered in the 1937 All-Star Game. He substantially pitched in only nine big-league seasons (1932–1940) and was done by the time he reached 30 years of age. He tried to pitch in 1941, but that lasted one inning. At age 37, he pitched four innings for the St. Louis Browns in 1947, but that was little more than a stunt.

Still, Dean was elected to the National Baseball Hall of Fame in 1953 and when the Cardinals opened their team Hall of Fame in 2014, he was in the inaugural class. The reason is simple—there has never been anyone quite like him.

From 1932 to 1936, he was arguably the best pitcher in the game. In that five-year stretch, he had 120 of his 150 career wins. In 1934, Ol' Diz's younger brother Paul Dean joined the Cardinals. Dizzy bragged about his little brother's skills and boldly predicted "me and Paul" would combine to win 45 games. Dizzy won 30 that season. "Daffy," as Dizzy liked to call Paul, won 19 for a total of 49.

The Cardinals won the pennant and faced the Detroit Tigers in the World Series. Once more, Dean let loose the braggadocios, assuring everyone he and his kid brother would pitch the Redbirds past the Tigers. Once again, he was right. The Dean brothers each won two World Series games and the Cardinals won a memorable series in seven.

Meanwhile, the uncultured charm of the Deans, the gritty determination of Martin and his "Gas House Gang" teammates, captured the imagination of working-class Americans, who were fighting to overcome their Depression-era challenges.

When it was all said and done, Dizzy Dean led the National League in wins (30), shutouts (7), and strikeouts (195) in 1934. He was named the National League Most Valuable Player.

He would finish second in the MVP balloting each of the next two seasons, winning 28 games in 1935 and 24 more in '36. Since that magical 1934 season, 81 baseball seasons have come and gone. But there has yet to be another National League pitcher to win as many as 30 games.

But the beauty of the movie *The Pride of St. Louis* is that it captures more than Dean's baseball credits. It does a decent job of capturing his unbridled, country-boy confidence and flair. You get plenty of Dizzy Dean, the seed-throwing backbone and mouthpiece of the hard-nosed Cardinals. But you get even more of Dizzy Dean, the Arkansas son of sharecroppers. You see him as an incorrigible braggart, a fun-loving showman, and a humble soul.

Herman H. Mankiewicz wrote the script and Harmon Jones directs. Actor Dan Dailey plays Dean with the appropriate Huckleberry Finn–esque accents and blowhard expressions. Dean comes across as a raw talent, an insufferable clown, and, at the core, a sentimental lug.

The film was released in 1952, a year before Dean was ushered into Cooperstown. As you might expect, it has plenty of clichés, sappy dialog, and predictable circumstances. It also takes a few liberties with the truth, but Dean didn't care.

When 20th Century Fox gave him a fat check for the rights to his story, he said, "Jeez, they're gonna give me 50,000 smackers just fer livin'!"

And as campy baseball movies go, it's not a bad flick. The script pays attention to Dean's focus on the parallel career of his little brother, Paul, who also flamed out early. After winning 38 games for the Cardinals from 1934 to 1935, Paul Dean won only 12 more games in a nine-year career.

But the brothers Dean were a phenomenon and Richard Crenna does well playing the tag-along part of Paul. Joanne Dru has a nice supporting role as Dizzy Dean's wife, Patricia. Dru would go on to become the real-life aunt of former Cubs first baseman Pete LaCock.

Dean's St. Louis friend Johnny Kendall is handled by Richard Hylton, and Hugh Sanders plays the scout who finds him. Also of note, longtime network news broadcaster Chet Huntley plays the part of sportscaster Tom Weaver and Stuart Randall plays Frankie Frisch.

The movie has an unusual ending. Rather than the stereotypical triumphant moment in a dramatic game, the story concludes with Dean at the end of the line. His playing career over, he re-emerges as a broadcaster, describing baseball as only he might. But the liberties he takes with grammar draw the ire of St. Louis school teachers.

In an ending that tugs at the heart, Ol' Diz wins them over.

It is worth remembering Dean for at least one other moment. In 1948, cancer-stricken Babe Ruth was making what amounted to a farewell tour of major league ballparks. In June, he came to Sportsman's Park in St. Louis, where Dean was supposed to pitch to him. As the thin, weakened Ruth stepped to the plate, the bat dropped off his shoulder.

Sensing the awkwardness of the situation, Dean stepped off the mound, walked to the plate, turned and pointed to right field, where Ruth once hit three home runs during a 1926 World Series game. The pantomime gave Ruth a chance to gather himself and saved the moment.

See a Springfield Cardinals Texas League Game in Springfield, Missouri

WHERE: Hammons Field, 955 E. Trafficway Street, Springfield, MO 65802

WHEN: 70 home dates between April and September from which to choose

WHAT TO DO: Purchase tickets to a Springfield Cardinals game, 417-863-2143 or www.springfieldcardinals.com. Regular ticket-office hours at Hammons Field are 9:00 AM to 5:00 PM, Monday through Friday. When the Cardinals play at home on Saturdays and Sundays, the ticket office opens at 10:00 AM. On game days, the ticket office remains open through game time. The Hammons Field gates open one hour prior to game time.

If need be, book a hotel in Springfield, Missouri. There are several to choose from. University Plaza Hotel (417-864-7333; www.upspringfield .com) is within walking distance of Hammons Field and offers a "fan discount" rate of some $109 per night.

COST: Tickets to a Springfield Cardinals Class AA Texas League game run between $7 and $28, depending on how crazy you want to get. A room at a local hotel could cost anywhere from $40 to $199 a night, again, depending on your needs.

BUCKET RANK: 🪣🪣🪣

There is something about seeing baseball on a slightly less pretentious scale, something organic, something genuine, something promising. Professional baseball has a rich history in Springfield, dating all the way back to the 1887 Springfield Indians of the Southwestern League.

The Queen City of the Ozarks has played host to numerous teams over the years, and has gone through long periods without a team at all. But while the 1929 and 1930 Springfield Midgets were affiliated with the American League St. Louis Browns, much of Springfield's baseball heritage is connected to the National League Cardinals, still located some 215 miles northeast on I-44.

In 1931, the St. Louis Cardinals purchased a Class C farm team and relocated it to Springfield. That team went to the playoffs numerous times and won five Western Association titles—1931, '32, '34, '37, and '39. During the period, some of the greatest Cardinals ever to play came through Springfield, including brothers Dizzy and Paul Dean, slugging Joe Medwick, and popular Peppar Martin.

In 1941, Stan "the Man" Musial played for Springfield. It was Musial's first season after he hurt his throwing arm and had to give up pitching—and boy, did he struggle. As a full-time Springfield outfielder, Musial batted .379 with 27 doubles, 10 triples, 26 home runs, 94 RBIs, and 100 runs in 87 games.

Of course, with numbers like that, he didn't stay long. Musial was promoted to Class AAA Rochester during the season and, before the summer ended, all the way to the major leagues. The rest is Hall of Fame history.

Before the 2005 season, the Cardinals ended an association with the Class AA Tennessee Smokies of the Southern League and purchased the El Paso Diablos of the Texas League. They moved the team to Springfield.

That spring, the Springfield Cardinals christened Hammons Field by playing the parent St. Louis Cardinals in an exhibition. Musial was on hand to throw out the first pitch and play "Take Me Out to the Ball Game" on his harmonica. A crowd of nearly 12,000 attended.

Stan stumbled a bit upon throwing the ceremonial pitch, but Springfield general manager Matt Gifford was there to keep "the Man" from falling. Hey, what do you want? He gave up pitching in 1940.

Since that time, some 70 players have passed through Springfield on their way to the big-league roster. If you've been to a game at the inviting ballpark, chances are you secured an autograph from one of those players.

Each night at Hammons Field, several players are stationed at the entrance gates to greet fans and sign autographs the ballpark opens. Players are also sometimes available by the home dugout on the first-base side before and after the game, available to sign as time permits.

Hammons Field is often listed among the best ballparks in the minor leagues for its family-friendly atmosphere, and is among the best attended. Attendance at Springfield Cardinals games has averaged nearly 6,500 since the ballpark opened.

Perhaps you'll want to buy a souvenir to remember the experience. Some of the fan apparel items are retro looking and the Springfield Cardinals store is located at the ballpark. The deck on top of the Cardinals' dugout has the championship banners from the 1930s.

The Springfield Cardinals' best season was 2012, when they finished first in the North Division in the second half of the season and captured the Texas League Championship. They defeated the Tulsa Drillers 3–2 in a best-of-five divisional playoff series, then defeated the Frisco Rough Riders 3–1 in a best-of-five championship series. Current Cardinals Kolten Wong, Carlos Martinez, Trevor Rosenthal, and Xavier Scruggs were part of that team.

Take a Busch Stadium Tour and See Trinket City

WHERE: 700 Clark Ave., St. Louis, MO 63102

WHEN: Stadium tours are offered twice a day during the off-season, at 11:00 AM and 12:30 PM. During the season they are conducted at 9:30 AM, 11:00 AM, 12:30 PM, and 2:00 PM. Tours are not offered during home day games and some special events.

WHAT TO DO: Purchase a ticket to a Busch Stadium Tour, or a combo ticket for an additional tour of the Cardinals Hall of Fame Museum.

COST: Single tickets range from $8 for children (15 and under), $10 for seniors, and $12 for adults. Combo tickets are $14, $16, and $18, respectively. Children three years old and under are free.

BUCKET RANK:

The Cardinals conduct tours of the ballpark all year long, come rain or shine. Fans make a half-mile trek through the home of their favorite team, accessing areas they are not allowed in when attending a game. The hour-long expedition visits the radio press box, the players' clubhouses, and just about everywhere in between.

You'll have a chance to snap a picture with the World Series trophies, sit in the dugout, take the field, and imagine what it's really like be a Cardinal. It's all inviting stuff, but one of the highlights is Marty Hendin's Trinket City.

The former Cardinals vice president of community relations, Hendin was a hoarder of all things Cardinals. During his 35 years with the team, spent largely in public relations and marketing, he usually handled the duties of greeting and taking care of first-pitch and anthem-singing dignitaries at the ballpark. He also had his hand in many club promotions and giveaways.

Hendin was an unabashed fan and shameless enthusiast when it came to the Cardinals and collecting pieces of his experience. Once housed in his office and his home, his remarkable collection is now on display at Busch Stadium III in Trinket City, located on the lower concourse behind home plate and the field-level seats.

There is also a satellite Trinket City located on the first floor of the Millennium Student Center at the University of Missouri–St. Louis, from which Hendin graduated before joining the Cardinals. There, a sign explained the display: "Welcome to Trinket City. Stop by. Take in the sights. And remember who built the place. If you didn't know Marty Hendin, get to know him there."

At the stadium, the memorabilia is displayed in a large glass case, with photograph collages adorning the walls on each side. Hendin had his picture taken with presidents, admirals, actresses, rock stars, ballerinas, and ballplayers. From Stan Musial to Sammy Hagar, Muhammad Ali to Marie Osmond, all are present and accounted for.

Former Cardinals owner August "Gussie" Busch is artistically rendered in a golden frame; Mr. T is depicted in golden chains. Pepper Martin is there, and so is Pia Zadora. Anyone who is anyone—that is, anyone who has thrown out a ceremonial pitch, sung the national anthem or visited the stadium, or otherwise had the occasion to shake hands and take a photo with Hendin—now permanently resides in Trinket City.

Of course, it isn't all photos taken at the stadium. You have your 1949 *Time* magazine cover of Stan the Man; your autographed reproduction of the 1968 *Sports Illustrated* photo with Roger Maris, Tim McCarver, Bob Gibson, Lou Brock, Curt Flood, and more; and your Danbury

MARTY HENDIN

There's an expression people use these days. Ask them what they're up to and they'll say, "Oh, you know, livin' the dream."

When Marty Hendin said that, it wasn't just an expression; it was true. As he would tell you, Hendin was just a big kid from St. Louis, nobody special, living a dream.

Hendin grew up in St. Louis County and went to University City High School, the same school that produced big league players like Ken Holtzman, Art Shamsky, Bernard Gilkey, and longtime Cardinals General Manager Bing Devine. But Hendin was never an athlete to speak of; he just loved athletics.

After graduating U. City High, he went to the University of Missouri–St. Louis and became the first sportswriter on UMSL's student newspaper, the *Current*. When he wasn't covering the Rivermen, he also distinguished himself—and perhaps set his path in life—by establishing UMSL's first spirit club, the Steamers.

Hendin graduated from UMSL with a business degree and found a job with the Cardinals in 1973. Over the next 35 years he worked his way up through the organization, starting in media relations and graduating to vice president of community relations.

As part of his duties, he became the club liaison for celebrities and dignitaries throwing out ceremonial first pitches before games. As a result, he came to know and have pictures taken with a wide variety of famous figures, from Bob Hope to Mr. T, from President Barack Obama to Mickey Mouse.

Hendin is also credited with creating the club's mascot, Fredbird. The anthropomorphic cardinal made his debut with the club in 1979, but

Hendin was quick to point out that he was just one of several people involved in hatching the bird.

"Everyone wants to credit me with inventing him, and I didn't," Hendin once said. "He was sort of put under my wing, so to speak... Basically, the idea had been broached by many different people. That was the heyday of the San Diego Chicken, and a number of clubs were adopting the mascot concept."

Now, that's his official resume. Less officially—and perhaps most important—the big galoot became the spiritual savant of the franchise, a tireless worker for all things promoting the Cardinals and raising money for charities in the community.

Most importantly, he was the founding father and all-powerful mayor of Trinketville. From day one of his time with the Cardinals, Hendin began cherishing and collecting every trinket, bauble, photograph, stadium giveaway, personal keepsake, and piece of memorabilia associated with the Cardinals.

As he collected each article, Hendin displayed it in his stadium office, sitting atop his deck, mounted on the walls, hanging from the ceiling, strewn all over the floor. It got to the point where one could hardly enter the cluttered room without disrupting some type of Cardinals adornment.

Of course, that's to say nothing of his residence, which had a similar motif. Housekeepers still lie awake at night just thinking about it.

Marty Hendin was 6'4", somewhat heavyset, wearing horn-rim frames and thick glasses. There was nothing about him that suggested royalty. But he felt like royalty. He thought being part of Cardinals baseball was magical, and he wanted as many people as possible to share the experience.

"If anyone had told me when I was growing up that I would be doing what I am doing today...I would never have believed it, " he once said in an interview. "That I know people like Stan Musial and Tony

La Russa and have met presidents and rock stars and movie stars is amazing. There's no such thing as a dull day. Every time that phone rings, it's an adventure."

Hendin and his collection became an institution within the institution and one of the biggest challenges the club faced when it moved from Busch Stadium II to its new stadium in 2006 built next door was transferring all the articles in Trinket City.

Hendin was gone much too quickly. He passed away from cancer in 2008 at the age of 59. But his incredible spirit lives on in Trinket City— the Cardinals have made sure of that.

Mint statuette of Lou Brock stealing one of his 938 bases, among other things.

That's to say nothing of the bobblehead collection, where anyone who has had a head at Busch Stadium, and had it bobbled, is part of the show. Hall of Fame induction pins also are prevalent, as well as All-Star Game pins and World Series pins.

Some of Hendin's personal favorite items include "Lenard Blaine," an unopened Cabbage Patch Kid dressed in Cardinals home whites; a bat made to look like it's covered with pine tar and signed by George Brett; a harmonica signed by Musial; and a CD cover signed by Bruce Springsteen.

Next to Trinket City at the ballpark is the Marty Hendin First Pitch Room, or the green room for dignitaries on hand to do the honors. On the walls of the room are pictures of those who have handled the duties in the past, including a photo of president George W. Bush in a red Cardinals jacket, tossing out the initial serving of the 2004 season on April 5, 2004.

Also there is President Barack Obama, wearing his black Chicago White Sox jacket, firing the first seed for the MLB All-Star Game at Busch Stadium III on July 14, 2009. Asked about the jacket, the president said everyone knows he's a big White Sox fan. Besides, he added, "My wife thinks I look cute in this jacket."

Perhaps the most interesting picture is the antiquated photograph of President William Howard Taft attending a Cardinals game at Robison Field in St. Louis in 1910. Taft was the first president to throw out a first pitch, which he had done to open the season in Washington earlier that summer. He dropped in at Robison Field to catch the Cardinals, but when that game turned lopsided, he left early to catch the American League St. Louis Browns game, a few blocks away at Sportsman's Park.

Taft once called the game of baseball "a clean, straight game and it summons to its presence everybody who enjoys clean, straight athletics."

Those are words to live by in Trinket City.

* *

Witness a Cardinals No-Hitter

The Cardinals have orchestrated only 10 no-hit games in their long and illustrious history. There has yet to be a Cardinals no-hitter pitched at Busch Stadium III, which opened on April 10, 2006. The good news is there has yet to be an opposition no-hitter at the stadium, as well.

Officially, Major League Baseball recognizes a no-hitter "when a pitcher (or pitchers) retires each batter on the opposing team during the entire course of a game, which consists of at least nine innings." There was a time when no-hitters of less than nine innings were recognized by the league as official. That was changed to its current form in 1991.

No-hitters are rare enough that six major league teams have had one or fewer in their history. The San Diego Padres have never had a no-hit win. Keep in mind, a perfect game represents a subcategory of no-hitter and is especially rare. The Cardinals have never pitched a perfect game, which is defined by MLB as occurring when "no batter reaches any base during the course of the game."

And, by the way, a no-hitter does not represent a guaranteed win. Five times in major league history, a team has held an opponent to no hits and lost. The most recent occurrence took place in 2008, when the Dodgers beat the Angels 1–0 without the benefit of a single hit.

Oh, the humanity!

Unofficially, it is taboo in major league dugouts to speak of a no-hitter as it becomes a real possibility. As for broadcasters, some honor the code, some don't. Legendary Los Angeles Dodgers broadcaster Vin Scully has called 23 no-hit games in his career. When he called Clayton Kershaw's gem in 2014, Scully made numerous references to the fact that Kershaw had allowed no hits.

"We don't believe in superstition," Scully said on the air. "Our job is to give you information."

As noted, depending on how far back you want to go, the Cardinals claim 10 no-hitters. Only four have been thrown in front of a St. Louis crowd, and that's counting a no-no tossed by Ted Breitenstein on October 4, 1891.

Breitenstein, a St. Louis native, was a part-time outfielder and relief pitcher that season. Manager Charlie Comiskey allowed the rookie left-hander to make his first major league start on the final day of the season, the first game of a doubleheader with the Kentucky Colonels.

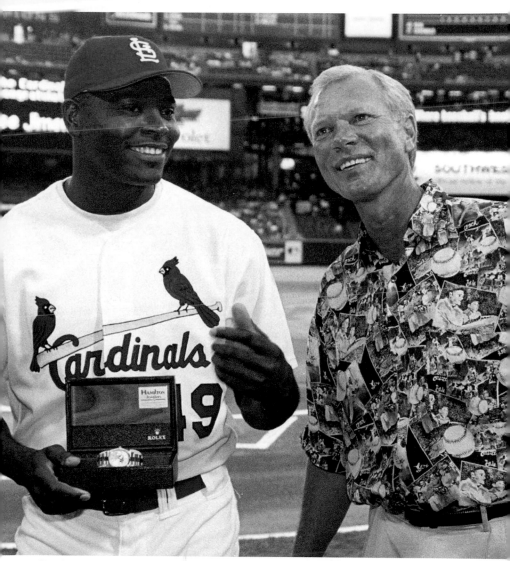

Cardinals pitcher Jose Jimenez (left) was honored for pitching a no-hitter against the Arizona Diamondbacks on June 25, 1999. Bob Forsch (right) threw two no-hitters in his time with the club.

BOB FORSCH

There have been two former Cardinals pitchers to have multiple no-hitters: Bob Forsch and Ted Breitenstein. But Breitenstein pitched the second of his two no-hitters as a member of the Cincinnati Reds.

Forsch is the only player in club history to pitch multiple no-hitters for the Cardinals, and he pitched both of them at home. Bob's brother Ken Forsch also pitched a no-hitter as a member of the Houston Astros. They are the only brothers in major league history to accomplish that family double.

The first of Bob Forsch's no-hitters came on April 16, 1978, and it is remembered as one of the more controversial no-hitters in big-league history. The 6'4" right-hander pitched brilliantly, no question. He walked two and struck out three in the game.

However, in the top of the eighth inning, a third Phillies batter reached base under controversial circumstances. Garry Maddox pulled a ground ball past third baseman Ken Reitz and into left field. The official scorer for the game was Neal Russo, a longtime Cardinals beat writer for the *St. Louis Post-Dispatch*. Russo felt Reitz had a play on the ball and failed to make it. He unhesitatingly ruled the play an error on Reitz, keeping the no-hitter intact.

Forsch induced a double-play grounder from the next batter, Bob Boone, then retired the last four Phillies to complete the no-hitter.

It was the first home-team no-hitter in St. Louis since Jesse Haines achieved the feat against the Braves—also a 5–0 score—on July 17, 1924. It was the first no-hitter by a Cardinals pitcher anywhere since Bob Gibson had no-hit the Pirates 11–0 in Pittsburgh on August 14, 1971.

After Forsch's no-no was complete, the Phillies made it clear they felt it was also bogus. They criticized Russo's ruling.

"Base hit all the way," Phillies manager Danny Ozark told Russo. "Reitz didn't even touch the ball."

Philadelphia third baseman Mike Schmidt chimed in: "Forsch pitched a dazzling one-hitter."

Right fielder Bake McBride was a former Cardinal and knew Forsch well. But even McBride was astounded by the scoring of Maddox's grounder. "We almost all fell off the bench when the call was made," McBride said.

But Russo never wavered. "I thought Reitz should have had it," he told the Associated Press. "I called it immediately. It was an ordinary play, maybe a step to Reitz's left. The ball wasn't hit that hard. There was no doubt in my mind."

Russo then accused the Phillies of sour grapes. "Of course, the Phillies, to a man, argued. But that's human nature," he said.

As for Reitz, "the Zamboni" backed Russo's assessment. "I thought the ball was hit a lot harder than it was," he said. "When I went for the ball, I double-pumped and when I came up with the glove the second time, the ball hit the webbing and went by me. I make that play 99 out of 100 times. This was the 100th time. It was an error all the way."

Thirty-four years later, the Cardinals would be on the other side of the ledger. On June 1, 2012, Johan Santana pitched the first no-hitter in the history of the New York Mets franchise, beating the Cardinals 8–0. During the game, a drive by Cardinals center fielder Carlos Beltran was ruled foul by third-base umpire Adrian Johnson. Replays showed the ball landed fair on the outfield chalk.

That disputed call led to suggestions for more instant-replay review and prompted the *St. Louis Post-Dispatch* to attach an asterisk to the achievement.

As for Forsch, as if to put the argument to bed and prove it was no fluke, he pitched a second no-hitter at Busch Stadium on September 26, 1983, beating the Montreal Expos 3–0. There were no controversial rulings involved.

Forsch won 20 games in 1977, going 20–7, and finished his 16-year career with a record of 168–136. Originally drafted as a third baseman, he also batted .213 and had 12 home runs during his career, and was twice the National League Silver Slugger winner as the league's best-hitting pitcher (1980, 1987).

And if you needed someone to win a game at Busch Stadium II, he was your man. Forsch won more games than any other pitcher at the old stadium, going 93–60 with a 3.41 earned run average.

Forsch was inducted into the Cardinals Hall of Fame, along with Simmons, Curt Flood, and George Kissell, in August 2015.

Breitenstein faced the minimum 27 batters, allowing one walk in an 8–0 shutout.

Not only was it the first no-hitter in franchise history, it was the last no-hitter thrown in the old American Association, which folded after that season. The Cardinals were known as the Browns in 1891. They would change their name to the Perfectos in 1899 and the Cardinals in 1900. Also keep in mind the pitching distance from the pitcher's box to home plate was 50 feet at that time, not the current 60', 6".

It should be pointed out that the American League St. Louis Browns pitched three additional no-hitters in St. Louis, the last by rookie Bobo Holloman in 1953. Like Breitenstein, Holloman was making his first major league start. So if you're making your first major league start and you're hoping for a no-hitter, St. Louis is your best bet.

After Breitenstein's masterpiece, the Cardinals waited almost 33 years before experiencing another no-hitter, their longest period without that pleasure. On July 17, 1924, Jesse "Pop" Haines beat the Boston Braves 5–0 on a no-hitter at Sportsman's Park.

St. Louis then waited more than 53 years to witness its next home no-hitter. Bob Forsch ended the drought by shutting out the Philadelphia Phillies 5–0 on April 16, 1978. It is the earliest calendar date for a no-hitter in franchise history. It also was the second Cardinals no-hitter caught by catcher Ted Simmons, who had been at the opposite end of Bob Gibson's 11–0 no-hitter at Pittsburgh on August 14, 1971.

Simmons is the only player in Cardinals history to catch two no-hitters. Former Boston Red Sox catcher Jason Varitek has the major league record of catching four no-hitters.

In that same context, Forsch pitched a second no-hitter at Busch Stadium on September 26, 1983—this time with Darrell Porter catching. Forsch beat the Montreal Expos 3–0 to become the only pitcher in club history to throw multiple no-hitters and the last to pitch one in St. Louis. That means the Cardinals were 2–0 in no-hitters at Busch Stadium II. During its 40-year existence (1966–2005), the team never lost a no-hitter at the hubcap-shaped park.

For the record, the Cardinals have been no-hit victims eight times in their history, most recently in an 8–0 loss to Mets lefty Johan Santana in New York on June 1, 2012. Oddly enough, the St. Louis Browns were also no-hit losers eight times.

Chapter 6

Things to Know

Cardinals great Stan Musial, playing his trusty harmonica, leads the audience in singing "Take Me Out to the Ball Game" during National Baseball Hall of Fame induction ceremonies in 2005.

Learn To Play "Take Me Out to the Ball Game" on the Harmonica

In Europe, the harmonica is properly known as a "mouth organ" or "mouth harp." In America, it's sometimes referred to in less sophisticated terms, such as the "pocket piano." That description is especially appropriate where Stan Musial is concerned, because he almost always had a 10-hole diatonic harmonica in his pocket, at the ready.

Like Abraham Lincoln, Dwight D. Eisenhower, and Ronald Reagan before him, Musial became hooked on the harmonica.

"I first started learning the harmonica as a kid," Musial said. "It's not hard to play. But like anything, you've got to practice. When I was playing baseball, I never played much. I didn't know too many songs at that time."

In his post-playing career, it became one of his calling cards. Musial did not enjoy public speaking and often avoided honorary dinners or events where he would be required to make a speech. But the harmonica became a failsafe, a comfortable way to avoid monologues and connect with fans at such gatherings.

Musial loved to get a rise out of people in two ways—by telling jokes and playing his harmonica. In fact, baseball Commissioner Ford Frick might have done well to edit his famous remarks about Musial to read, "Here stands baseball's perfect warrior, here stands baseball's perfect knight...and here stands a harmonica player."

"I'm a musician," Musial once said with a smile. "I play harmonica for relaxation. A good way to relax and entertain people. An excellent way to have fun."

In the 1990s, Musial joined the Gateway Harmonica Club and played in a trio with music publishing legend Mel Bay and banjo virtuoso John Becker.

It became a tradition at the annual National Baseball Hall of Fame induction ceremonies for Musial to play "Take Me Out to the Ball Game." He became noted for other songs as well, as he regularly played the harmonica at baseball dinners and on other occasions.

Have harmonica, will play became his motto. Musial played with a number of well-known artists from various musical genres, including Al Hirt, Charlie Pride, Roy Clark, and the Eagles. In 1994, he joined St. Louis Symphony pops conductor Richard Hayman to perform a harmonica duet of the national anthem for the Cardinals' opener.

In 2001, he played "Take Me Out to the Ball Game" at the White House during a presentation of baseball Hall of Fame Players.

MEL BAY

Stan Musial had 3,630 hits on the baseball field during his big league career. But he was never regarded for his ability to teach hitting. As his former teammate Curt Flood once observed, Musial was a natural when it came to hitting. He could not explain it "any more than a hawk can explain how it flies."

But in 1994, Musial teamed up with guitarist and music-publishing giant Mel Bay to try teaching something else. That is, the two marketed an instructional cassette and beginner's book for the harmonica, entitled *Mel Bay Presents Stan Musial Plays the Harmonica*.

Like Musial, Bay was a legend, albeit in the music world. Born in Bunker, Missouri, Bay grew up in De Soto, some 50 miles south of St. Louis, where his parents owned a grocery store. In 1926, Bay got a Sears Roebuck guitar for Christmas and he couldn't put it down.

He taught himself to play and then learned to play tenor banjo, as well. Bay began playing with bluegrass bands in the Ozark hills and traveling medicine shows. By the early 1930s, he moved to St. Louis. He played professionally in local jazz bands and worked at radio stations.

At the same time, Bay began teaching and developing a chord system. That led to his first published book, *The Orchestral Chord System for Guitar*, in 1947. Bay opened a music retail store in downtown St. Louis and later in the suburb of Kirkwood. With his publishing proficiency, he provided instrumental instruction to generations of St. Louis music lovers and a foundation for musicians around the globe.

When they played in St. Louis, rock bands like the Eagles, the Who, and the Rolling Stones would visit the Mel Bay Music Center to pay homage to Bay. In 1996, he was honored by the Guitar Foundation of America with a concert at the Sheldon Theater. Bay died in 1997 at the age of 84.

A big baseball fan, Bay met Musial in his store one day and they became fast friends. In turn, they befriended four-string-banjo master John Becker, who had played gigs in the legendary St. Louis entertainment district of the 1950s, Gaslight Square.

With Musial on harmonica, they formed a trio and began performing at charity events, hospitals, and retirement homes, featuring what they referred to as "Geriatric Jazz."

Musial recalled one nursing-home session in particular: "I liked to close my eyes when I played, so I could concentrate on the notes," he said. "Well, we were doing a song and when I opened my eyes, half the people there were asleep."

He laughed: "So I played a little louder and woke them up."

Bay got the idea to draw on Musial's celebrity and publish an instructional package for the harmonica. The trio went into the studio and recorded an instructional cassette to be packaged with a Musial book of 58 songs for beginners.

Among the 58 tunes are classics like "On Top of Old Smokey," "Camptown Races," and "Meet Me in St. Louis, Louis"—and, of course, "Take Me Out to the Ball Game." The songbook includes pictures of Musial demonstrating how the harmonica should be held. There is also a page dedicated to Musial's career baseball records and photos of him on the field.

"He's an amateur player," Bay said, explaining the Musial song list. "One of the most difficult things was finding 58 songs without sharps or flats. But Stan doesn't have to be great. His personality and his fame makes it great. He can play a half-dozen songs and still make a hit record."

Technically speaking, Musial was a musician even before he became recognized for his harmonica playing. In the 1940s, the heyday of the "St. Louis Swifties" teams that won three world championship in five years, young Musial played the clubhouse coat hangers and slide whistle in informal jug-band sessions to celebrate wins.

"I never had the courage to try my harmonica outside my hotel room," he once said.

With that in mind, the Cardinals honored Musial on April 12, 2013, with a "Stan Musial Tribute Harmonica" night promotion at Busch Stadium.

As patrons entered the stadium, the team handed out 25,000 harmonicas, imprinted with Musial's signature, encased along with instructions on how to play "Take Me Out to the Ball Game." On the occasion, a new plaque was added to the Musial statue outside Gate 3 of the stadium and was dedicated with a Navy color guard on hand. Seaman First Class Musial served 15 months in the Navy at the end of World War II.

In addition, members of the Gateway Harmonica Club occupied each gate leading into the ballpark, providing fans with quick lessons as they entered. A special commemorative baseball was used for the game and many of Musial's children and grandchildren were on the field to throw out ceremonial first pitches.

Come the middle of the sixth inning—in honor of No. 6, of course—the stadium video board showed Musial leading the way, and the entire stadium, which included a gate of 42,528, joined in for a rendition of "Take Me Out to the Ball Game." Obviously befuddled, the visiting Milwaukee Brewers lost 2–0 to the Cardinals that night.

Even the Cardinals players—some of them armed with harmonicas in the dugout—got into the spirit of the evening.

"I had the great fortune to be able to meet him last year in person," said Cardinals outfielder Carlos Beltran, "and it was one of the highlights of my career."

Cardinals manager Mike Matheny recalled meeting Stan "the Harmonica Man" Musial at a wedding both attended in 1991.

"Stan came over on his own and talked to me and 30 minutes later, he still was treating me like I was something special," said Matheny, who was a minor league catcher at the time of the encounter. "It was pretty unforgettable."

Matheny recalled that the band that was hired to provide entertainment at the reception hardly unpacked their instruments. Musial pulled out his "pocket piano" and took over.

"Nobody was about to ask him to get off the stage," said Matheny.

A Stan Musial Harmonica Night promotion also was held in June 2013 at Roger Dean Stadium in Jupiter, Florida, home of the club's spring training operations and the Palm Beach Cardinals. In 1998, Musial played "Take Me Out to the Ball Game" during the seventh-inning stretch of the inaugural game at Roger Dean Stadium.

Learn to Score the Cardinal Way

Believe it or not, there is a "Cardinal Way" to score a baseball game. That may sound a bit pretentious, even arrogant. But in truth it is simply a uniform language used by the organization's personnel so the information is discernible, regardless of who is keeping it and who is reading it. In other words, it has kept everyone on the same page since being instituted back in the 1940s.

Pablo Picasso once said of painting, "it is just another way of keeping a diary." He could have been talking about keeping a scorecard. The record-keeping practice lends itself to ingenuity, creativity, and proprietary elements. It can be a window to the past or a picture for the future. It can be universal and it can be personal.

Paul Dickson, author of *The Joy of Keeping Score: How Scoring the Game Has Influenced and Enhanced the History of Baseball*, explains the power of the scorecard:

"A neighbor had a score sheet from the last game between the New York Giants and Brooklyn Dodgers," Dickson explains. "He recalled the whole game inning by inning, just looking at the scorecard. It was almost like watching a rabbi read scripture. Here he was recalling the whole game. It was kind of magic. It's sort of an analog thing you do in the digital age."

Henry Chadwick (October 5, 1824–April 20, 1908) is credited with inventing the practice of keeping a baseball score. The English-born Chadwick was a sportswriter, historian, and statistician who edited the first baseball guide sold to the public. He has also been credited with creating the baseball box score, which was adapted from a cricket scorecard as a means of reporting the particulars of a game.

The first baseball box score appeared in 1859. Chadwick's version was a grid with nine rows for players and nine columns for innings. It also used abbreviations, such as "K" for a strikeout, with "K" being the last letter of "struck" in "struck out." Chadwick was also the first to assign numbers to each defensive position for the purpose of keeping score.

Over the years, scorecards became quite desirable for their covers, which often featured a picture of a star player or an illustration. The Cardinals honor that tradition by turning the annual cover for the scorecard sold at Busch Stadium into a work of art. St. Louis native and illustrator Mike Right has been designing the scorecard since 2003.

"I've always been a fan of the scorecards from the 1950s," Right said. "I loved the bird that they had back then and I always loved to draw in that retro style. So we got together and we tried to come up with a new bird that could that could be memorable and be a keepsake for years, to carry on that tradition. "

Right starts out drawing a cover idea in a thumbnail. Once he settles on the concept, he gets out the bigger pencils and does a full-scale sketch. He then copies the project into his computer, traces over it and adds the coloring.

THE "CARDINAL WAY GAME"

Each Cardinals scorecard comes with instructions on how to score the "Cardinal Way." It also gives you an example of what a Cardinal Way scorecard would look like, providing a glossary of symbols and notations and employing examples from an imaginary game.

For that purpose, the Cardinal Way employs quite the imaginary lineup: Lou Brock starts in left field and leads off; Rogers Hornsby plays second and bats second; Stan Musial patrols center field and bats third; Johnny Mize is at first base and in the cleanup spot; Enos Slaughter is in right field, batting fifth; Ken Boyer is stationed at third, batting sixth; Ted Simmons does the catching and bats seventh; Ozzie Smith is the shortstop and bats eighth; Bob Gibson is the starting pitcher, batting ninth.

Cardinals broadcaster Jack Buck had a good way to describe such a lineup: "That's a winner!"

It is interesting to note the Cardinals score twice in the first inning on the Cardinal Way example. Brock singles and advances to second on Hornsby's infield single. Brock then steals third before scoring on Musial's single.

Now, in 1974, when Brock broke Maury Wills' existing stolen-base record and swiped 118, Brock stole third only six times. So one might make a notation in one's Cardinal Way scoring that this was a rare steal by the "Base Burglar." It was also worth noting that Stan "the Cardinal Way Man" batted 1.000 with runners in scoring position.

Hornsby advances to third on Musial's hit, then scores on a sacrifice fly to center by Mize. Cardinal Way Mize thus ties Musial for the team lead in runs batted in. Slaughter is next and bounces into an inning-ending double play.

The example doesn't identify the opponent, which makes it impossible to say whether Slaughter stepped on Jackie Robinson's foot as he crossed the first-base bag.

In the second inning, Boyer reaches on an error by the first baseman. This leads one to believe the Cardinal Way lineup might be facing the Pittsburgh Pirates and Pedro Alvarez is playing first base. Alvarez had 23 errors at the position during the 2015 season.

Boyer advances to second on a wild pitch. The 6'1" 195-pound "Captain" did run well for his size, even stealing 22 bases one season, so this makes perfect sense.

What happens next is odd—Yadier Molina pinch-hits for Simmons. Now, Simmons batted .298 over his 13 years in St. Louis, with 172 home runs and 929 RBIs. Moreover, he was a switch-hitter, one of the best in the history of the game. For his career, he batted .287 against right-handed pitchers and .281 against lefties.

So it is hard to imagine circumstances that would call for Molina to pinch-hit for Simmons. Perhaps Cardinal Way "Simba" sustained some type of injury. On the other hand, Molina is a multiple Gold Glove–winning defender. It's a bit early to make such a move in the second inning, but with a two-run lead and Gibson pitching, maybe it's a move for defense.

Anyway, Molina flies out to left field in foul territory and Boyer stays at second. At this point, with Ozzie Smith up next, the opposition makes a pitching change. Again, Smith was a switch-hitter who had essentially the same success from each side during his career, batting .264 from the left side, .257 from the right.

Perhaps the Cardinal Way opponent was guarding against the possibility of a home run. Smith hit 23 batting right-handed in his career, but only five from the left side. This leads me to believe the Cardinal Way opposing starter might be Rick Rhoden.

"The Wizard" batted .377 over 77 career at-bats against Rhoden. With a runner on second, already trailing 2–0, the Cardinal Way opponent probably goes to the bullpen and brings in left-hander Frank Viola. Smith batted just .108 with no RBIs in 37 career at-bats against Viola.

Sure enough, Smith pops out to second. Gibson then grounds out to first, unassisted. There is no mention of a double switch by the Cardinal Way opponent during the pitching change. But given this entry, you have to think there might have been one.

And that's it for the Cardinal Way scorecard: two at-bats for the Cardinals, a 2–0 win. There is no mention of time of game, but it has to be about 20 minutes.

In addition to Right's outstanding illustrations, each scorecard comes with instructions on how to keep score the "Cardinal Way." Former Cardinals public relations director Jim Toomey was the originator of the method. The Cardinals now keep a written and digital record of each game.

The record-keeping duty usually falls on director of communications Melody Yount. But it can change from game to game, or road trip to road trip. If her other duties call Yount away for some reason, or if another member of the staff makes a road trip with the team, the team's way of scoring is employed and the information remains consistent. Those who read it can ascertain all the information they might need.

"One of the reasons we do it the way we do is that you can actually look at our scorecards, any game, back to the 1940s, and tell exactly what happened in that particular game, and re-create it," Yount said. "You can tell how a player advanced, and how he got to each position, if he stole a base, or who was batting when he stole that base.

"A lot of people keep score in a different way. It's all pretty much the same—somebody gets a hit and you write it down. We just have created a way that we do that to where you can tell where he hit the ball and how he got to each base, etc."

All you need is a sharp pencil...with an eraser.

. . . .

Learn to Do an Ozzie Smith Backflip

Next to Stan Musial, Osborne Earl "Ozzie" Smith might be the most popular player in the history of the St. Louis Cardinals franchise. And there are a number of reasons Cardinals fans identified with and embraced Smith.

He was a spectacular shortstop and one of the best defensive players—at any position—in the history of the game. He endeared himself to St. Louis fans with one acrobatic play after another while capturing a record 13 consecutive Gold Gloves in his career (1978–96). If you went to a game and Smith was playing, you almost certain to see him do something eye-opening.

At 5'11", 150 pounds, Smith was small in stature and big in heart, the kind of player fans naturally relate to and embrace as an overachiever. To his credit, Smith nurtured the notion.

For one, Smith took time before each game to sign autographs as he came off the field following pregame warmups. He also entertained fans during warmups by fielding ground balls from his knees and making no-look throws around the infield.

Cardinals shortstop Ozzie Smith does his signature backflip before Game 3 of the 1985 World Series between the Cardinals and the Kansas City Royals.

There was a legitimate purpose to the drills, as Smith prepared for any and every scenario. But he also appreciated the recreational value for fans in the stands.

And then...there was the flip.

Each season, both on Opening Day and on Fan Appreciation Day— the last home game of the season—No. 1 would sprint out of the dugout at Busch Stadium and perform a backflip on the way to his position. It became as much a tradition in St. Louis as the Clydesdales pulling the Budweiser beer wagon.

Smith once explained where the flip came from:

"At the end of spring training my first year with the Padres, we would do our running," Smith said. "Well, I didn't finish in the front of the pack. So some of the old guys, like Gaylord (Perry), Gene Tenace, and those guys said, "You're the youngest guy out here, you should be out front. So to show them I wasn't tired, I did (a backflip).

"Because (as a kid) I used to go to the trampolines on Thursdays and I used to live across the street from a wood factory, so I would go over and put planks between the stacks of wood and tumble into the sawdust.

"So that's really where I learned to do it and as a kid, it was always a dare thing with the other kids, you know, 'I dare you to do it,' to see whether or not you could do it. So it was just one of those things I could do."

On the final day of that 1978 season in San Diego, Tenace came up with the idea that Smith should do the flip as he took his position. Not wanting to be labeled a "hot dog," Smith declined. But when the Padres' public relations director got wind of it, he also asked Smith if he would do the flip to entertain the fans.

Smith finally relented. "Make a long story short, I did it, and they liked it so much, they asked me to do it on Opening Day the following year."

So when the Cardinals made the trade in December 1981 that sent shortstop Garry Templeton, outfielder Sixto Lezcano, and a player to be named later (pitcher Luis DeLeon) to the Padres in return for Smith, pitcher Steve Mura, and a player to be named later (pitcher Al Olmstead), they didn't just get a Hall of Fame shortstop, they got a signature backflip that captured the childlike exuberance and excitement that baseball holds for so many.

Mr. Smith even took his backflip to Tokyo. In November 1992, playing the series of All-Star Games between stars of the major leagues and stars of the Japanese League, Smith executed the trademark flip as he took the field. At the time he was a 37-year-old free agent and told reporters he would even consider playing in Japan if "somebody wanted to make it worth my while to come over here."

But he wound up signing a four-year deal to continue baseball and backflips in St. Louis until he retired in 1996. He entered the Hall of Fame in 2002.

Smith ended a 19-year career with 13 Gold Gloves, 15 All-Star selections, a shortstop-record 8,375 career assists, 2,460 hits, and 580 stolen bases. He also had an estimated major league record 37 backflips, starting with the end of the 1978 season through the end of the 1996 season.

And he never needed reminding about the backflips.

"I would have little old ladies come up to me and say, 'I know you, you're the one who does the flips.'" Smith recalled. "I would have to remind them that I played a little baseball, too."

Chapter 7

Things to Hear

Listen to Sam Bush's Song "The Wizard of Oz"

If you don't appreciate Ozzie Smith singing—as he does on the album *Oh Say Can You Sing?*—perhaps you'd appreciate hearing someone play and sing about him. Sam Bush does just that on his 2004 musical release, *King of My World*.

Bush grew up in Bowling Green, Kentucky, where he listened to Flatt and Scruggs on the Grand Ole Opry Show and listened to Cardinals baseball on KMOX Radio. As a teenager he was the national junior fiddle champion for three years running. But when he wasn't becoming a virtuoso instrumentalist on fiddle, mandolin, and guitar, he was a devoted fan of the Cardinals and baseball.

"I love baseball because it is unpredictable and there are no time limits," said Bush, now 63.

As a kid, he idolized players like Stan Musial, Bob Gibson, and Curt Flood. He would mimic Hall of Fame broadcasters Harry Caray and Jack Buck while playing in the yard. And as he got older, he embraced Ozzie Smith as his favorite.

He even named his German Shepherd mix "Ozzie" and played catch with him in the yard. "Ozzie" was also a wizard, as he lived to be 15 years old.

In 2004, Bush wrote a song for Smith and included it on a new album. There have been numerous artists who have written songs about baseball and players over the years, from the Beastie Boys to Bruce Springsteen. And John Fogerty's "Centerfield" might be the best-known baseball-inspired song of all.

But Bush's homage to Smith isn't just some corny tribute to his favorite player. It's a darn good song. It is a simple song, set to a country-swing cadence, that will have you tapping a toe and humming along soon after you hear it. You might even feel like doing a backflip at some point, although we recommend you consult with a physician before indulging in any strenuous physical activity. But the song does seem to fit, capturing the effervescence with which Smith played.

Here are the lyrics:

Hey Ozzie, Hey Ozzie
On the day after Christmas in '54
The greatest shortstop that every played before
He'd play the switch and that's a fact
He's the Wizard of Oz, there's no doubt about that

Hey Ozzie (Catch that ball)
Hey Ozzie (You're the best of all)
Osborne Earl now that's his name
Brought a brand new level to the game

Hey Ozzie, Hey Ozzie

The Cardinals knew they got a special gift
When he took the field with his backflip
Diving left and right, Soaring up and down
On the yellow brick road to Cooperstown

Hey Ozzie (Yeah catch that ball)
Hey Ozzie (You're the best of all)

The Wizard of Oz now that's his name
He's going to the Hall of Fame

Hey Ozzie, Hey Ozzie

Known for his fielding, he learned to hit
In the '85 playoffs, gave the Dodgers a fit
I sorta thought this was just a hoax
Cause Jack Buck said, "Go crazy, folks"

Hey Ozzie (Playoffs MVP)
Hey Ozzie (He'll bunt or he can take you deep)

By going up the middle he'll make you pay
By turning your head to a double play

Hey Ozzie, Hey Ozzie

"Frankie" Frisch, "Enos"
"Red" and "Dizzy"
Stan "the Man," Lou Brock and "Gibby"
They're making his plaque and etching his face
So the Wizard of Oz can take his place

Hey Ozzie (He's number one we love)
Hey Ozzie (He's got thirteen gold gloves)

He played in fifteen All-Star games
He's going to the Hall of Fame

Hey Ozzie, Hey Ozzie

Years later, on June 5, 2013, Bush got the thrill of meeting Smith for the first time. He threw out the first pitch of a Cardinals game with the Arizona Diamondbacks. And on hand to play catcher was none other than the "Wizard of Oz."

"Ozzie Smith is a hero of mine, and possibly the most gracious man that I've ever met," Bush said. "Sometimes dreams do come true. I'm the king of my world."

Bush even sees some similarities between playing bluegrass and playing baseball.

"The main similarity I see is in the work ethic," he once said. "Baseball players have to work hard to succeed. Bluegrass musicians work extremely hard, too."

Hear Bob Costas Refer to Ozzie Smith as a Power Hitter

There have not been many more popular sports figures in St. Louis than Osborne Earl Smith. He wore No. 1 in St. Louis for 15 seasons and makes his home there now. From his signature backflips to his acrobatic plays at shortstop, "The Wizard of Oz" was one of the most entertaining players ever to put on a big-league uniform.

He won 13 consecutive Gold Glove Awards. He was a National League All-Star 15 times. He had 2,460 hits and 580 stolen bases. He retired in 1996 with the most assists (8,375), most double plays (1,590), most total chances accepted (12,905), most years with 500 or more assists (eight), and most years leading the league in assists and chances accepted (eight).

But even by the biggest stretch of the imagination, there was one thing Smith was not—a power hitter. Only 499 of Smith's career blows went for extra bases. Only 28 were home runs.

In his career, Smith hit only five regular season home runs batting left-handed. He hit one, famously, in the postseason, winning Game 5 of the 1985 NLCS with his home run off Los Angeles right-hander Tom Niedenfuer.

But when you watch the Michael Ritchie–directed 1994 movie *The Scout*, you will be surprised to learn that Smith was considered a fearsome long-ball threat. It is a silly script to begin with. New York Yankees scout Al Percolo (Albert Brooks) discovers his "King Kong" playing baseball in Mexico. The mentally unstable prospect, Steve Nebraska (Brendan Fraser), has gone undiscovered, despite his ability to throw seeds and hit bombs. Percolo talks his bosses into offering Nebraska a contract, and that's when the nutty shenanigans begin.

The movie falls short in a number of ways. It came out in the fall of '94, or the same time of Major League Baseball's worst work stoppage. The World Series that year was canceled, except on the big screen.

Truth is, Hollywood hasn't made a lot of movies about the Cardinals, so any chance to see the Birds on the Bat on celluloid is worthwhile. And at the end of *The Scout*, you get your chance. After plenty of drama and hijinks, Nebraska gets to the big leagues and plays for the Yankees in the World Series.

As it turns out, in this particular Fall Classic, the opponent for the Pinstripes is none other than the Cardinals. That brings us to Game 7 and the final out at Yankee Stadium. As Nebraska battles his mental demons and prepares to close out the game for the Yankees, the final batter is Smith.

As Smith comes to the plate, the announcer, Costas, warns that Smith has been on a power surge as of late. In other words, he represents a threat to hit another home run. The year the movie came out—'94—Smith had three home runs.

What's more, he is facing Nebraska, a right-hander, so he takes his stance in the batter's box from the left side. Keep in mind, when Smith hit his "Go crazy, folks!" home run at Busch Stadium in 1985, he had gone more than 3,000 at-bats from the left side without hitting a home run.

In short, it was like casting Pee Wee Herman as Rocky Balboa. But hey, Costas didn't write it, he just read it.

Hear Ozzie Smith Sing "Cupid"

We all know Ozzie Smith could make a baseball glove sing. Smith won 13 Gold Gloves during his Hall of Fame career and played in 15 All-Star Games. And we knew his son, Nikko Smith, could sing. Nikko was a finalist and finished ninth in the fourth season of the television talent show *American Idol*. Nikko Smith also performed "The Star-Spangled Banner" at Busch Stadium prior to Game 4 of the 2006 World Series.

But who knew Pops also had pipes?

In May 2005, Good Sports released the album *Oh Say Can You Sing*, an exploration into the musical talents of a number of baseball players.

The CD featured 11 different players singing or rapping to a variety of different tunes. At the time of its release, 10 of the 11 were active players, with Smith being the only retired player and Hall of Fame Player in the session.

The set list looks like this:

1. Ben Broussard (Cleveland Indians): Vocals and guitar on U2's "With or Without You"

2. Sean Casey (Cincinnati Reds): Vocals on Toby Keith's "How Do You Like Me Now?"

3. Jeff Conine (Florida Marlins): Vocals on Stone Temple Pilots' "Plush"

4. Coco Crisp (Cleveland Indians): Rap on his original track "We Got That Thing"

5. Matt Ginter (New York Mets): Banjo on Dillard's "Dooley"

6. Aubrey Huff (Tampa Bay Devil Rays): Vocals on John Michael Montgomery's "Letters from Home"

7. Scott Linebrink (San Diego Padres): Vocals and guitar on Pat Green's "Wave on Wave"

8. Jimmy Rollins (Philadelphia Phillies): Rap on his original track "Wish List"

9. Ozzie Smith (Hall of Fame): Vocals on Sam Cooke's "Cupid"

10. Omar Vizquel (San Francisco Giants): Vocals and drums on the Goo Goo Dolls' "Broadway"

11. Kelly Wunsch (Los Angeles Dodgers): Vocals and guitar on John Mellencamp's "Hurts So Good"

Some quick observations: give Crisp and Rollins points for being savvy enough to record original material. Both are raps, which do not require nearly the vocal range of, say, Smith's choice.

What's more, an audience has never head "We Got That Thing" or "Wish List" before, which makes it difficult to judge Crisp or Rollins solely on the quality of his performance. You can decide easily enough whether you like the raps or not. But you can't say for sure if they have been delivered judiciously.

Also, points to Broussard, Wunsch, Linebrink, and Vizquel for playing instruments on their recordings. It demonstrates one of two things: either they are multiskilled, or they are extremely delusional about their playing abilities.

In the case of Broussard, however, it's an easy fit. He has released two solo albums and had one of his tunes, "Hold On to Me," used by a television show, *South of Nowhere*. As it turned out, the title was appropriate to the show, which wound up south of nowhere after 43 episodes (2005–2008).

Casey's "How Do You Like Me Now?" choice is interesting because he was one of the most well-liked players in baseball during his career, always approachable, always accommodating. It's worth mentioning that Casey makes a rather startling admission in the liner notes of the album, identifying Nick Lachey as one of his favorite artists. Other than a Lachey family member, who would do that?

Of all the challenges on the recording, you have to give credit to Smith for taking on Sam Cooke and "Cupid." Trying to cover an unforgettable song by an unforgettable tenor voice is basically laying yourself bare.

But like a pop-up throw from the hole, "the Wizard" pulls it off. His rendition of "Cupid" has a soulful flavor and is embellished with melancholy horns and a pleasing musical arrangement. Smith touches notes no one else on the album could hope to reach, and his song provides a refreshing offering to the mix.

So now, let's get this all straight. Ozzie Smith can play shortstop like no one else in the world. He can perform gymnastics and enter a baseball field doing backflips. *And* he can sing like Sam Cooke.

C'mon; that's just not fair.

The album gets a five-star review on Amazon, although there are only seven entries. One of them gives Smith high marks. Written under the handle of "Kingpin," it starts with "Holly [sic] crap they can sing!" and concludes,

"I was pleasantly suprised when I heard this CD. Because I was expecting a bunch of jocks giving us a reason to stick to their day jobs. But I was wrong. The best on here was Ben Broussard of the Indians because that boy can sing. Ozzie Smith though could sing pretty well to my suprise [sic]. So over all [sic] this CD is really good."

As you can see, Kingpin's spelling "suprisingly" is a little bit like Smith's performance and the CD itself—"suprising."

Hear Jack Buck's 9/11 Poem

It's safe to say everyone remembers where they were on the morning of Tuesday, September. 11, 2001. In a terrifying matter of moments, unspeakable acts took place in New York City, Pennsylvania, and Washington, D.C., that took the lives of some 3,500 and filled television screens with billowing black smoke and crumbled debris.

As a result of the terrorist attacks, Major League Baseball canceled games that day and extended the period through September 16. On September 17, with the nation still in a state of anger, heartbreak, and disbelief, games resumed. A way of life had to be reinstated; freedom and normalcy had to be restored.

Baseball, the professional world, and the entertainment world aspired to help people press through the sadness and outrage. There was no shame in it; there was only hope.

That night in St. Louis, the Cardinals prepared to take the field against the Milwaukee Brewers. Normally a "Sea of Red," the crowd of 32,563 became an ocean of red, white, and blue waving American flags.

Some 500 St. Louis firefighters and police officers took the field, lining the outfield warning track from foul line to foul line, paying homage to the many who lost lives responding to the attacks. A profound sadness filled the air, as eyes welled with tears and wounded spirits searched for therapeutic release.

Firefighters unfurled a gigantic flag in center field and a video tribute appeared on the scoreboard, accompanied by Lee Greenwood's patriotic song, "Proud to Be an American." The moment was chilling

Jack Buck read a poem he had written to honor the fallen firefighters and policemen of 9/11 during a pregame ceremony on September 17, 2001.

PICK A FAVORITE JACK BUCK CALL

Buck had many iconic calls and various fans have their favorites. On August 14, 1971, his voice cracked with emotion as he called the final out of Bob Gibson's no-hitter at Three Rivers Stadium in Pittsburgh: "And Gibson is one strike away from the no-hitter…he takes off his cap…he mops his brow…he looks in and gets the sign…he starts the windup…here's the pitch…and it's a strike called! A no-hitter for Gibson!"

On Sepember. 10, 1974, he was at the Busch Stadium microphone when Lou Brock broke the single-season stolen-base record with steal No. 105 against the Phillies: "Brock takes the lead…Ruthven checks him…he is…going! The pitch is a strike, the throw…he is there! He did it! 105 for Lou Brock!"

On October 14, 1985, he was at Busch Stadium when Ozzie Smith faced Los Angeles Dodgers right-hander Tom Niedenfuer in Game 5 of the National League Championship Series: "Smith corks one into right, down the line! It may go! Go crazy, folks! Go crazy! It's a home run! And the Cardinals have won the game…by the score of 3–2…on a home run by the Wizard! Go crazy!"

On October 16, 1985, Buck was in Los Angeles for Game 6 of the NLCS. The Cardinals trailed the Dodgers 5–4 in the ninth inning when Jack Clark faced Niedenfuer: "The Dodger right-hander is set and here's his pitch to Jack Clark…swing and a long one into left field…adios! Goodbye! And maybe that's a winner! A three-run homer by Clark and the Cardinals lead by the score of 7–5…and they may go to the World Series on that one, folks!"

Buck has also made some of baseball's most memorable calls to a national audience. Perhaps his best known came on October 15, 1988. He described what took place as injured pinch-hitter Kirk Gibson hobbled to the plate at Dodgers Stadium, his team trailing the Oakland A's 4–3 in the bottom of the ninth inning of World Series Game 1, a runner on and two outs: "Gibson...swings and a fly ball to deep right field...this is gonna be a home run....unbelievable! A home run for Gibson! And the Dodgers have won the game 5–4! I don't believe what I just saw!"

Another of Buck's best known calls came on October 26, 1991, when Kirby Puckett's 11th-inning home run won Game 6 for the Minnesota Twins and extended their 1991 World Series with the Atlanta Braves to a Game 7: "Into deep left center...for Mitchell...and we'll see you...tomorrow night!"

Joe Buck has followed in his father's footsteps to become the lead baseball, football, and now golf announcer for FOX Sports. Joe honored his dad while calling the 2011 World Series, under nearly identical circumstances to Puckett's heroics.

On October 27, 2011, Cardinals third baseman David Freese hit a solo homer in the bottom of the 11th inning to win Game 6 for St. Louis to beat Texas and send the series to Game 7. Like the Twins in '91, the Cardinals also won Game 7 to capture a dramatic world championship.

When Freese's drive landed over the center-field wall at Busch Stadium III, Joe described the moment: "We will see you tomorrow night!"

Not only was it the perfect call, but it was the perfect tribute to his beloved dad.

enough; then Jack Buck stepped to the microphone. An Army veteran and World War II Purple Heart recipient, the Hall of Fame broadcaster was adorned in a Cardinals-red blazer, embellished with an American flag pin on his lapel.

Buck would not live to see another September. The Parkinson's, diabetes, and other infirmities chipping away at his heath had gained a stronghold by this time. In less than three months he would enter the hospital and never come out.

He was shaking with tremors, awash in emotion, and unrelenting. Busch Stadium II fell silent. He reached into the pocket of his jacket, removed a piece of paper, and announced he had written a poem to read.

What followed was a moment of beauty, defiance, and reassurance that many Cardinals fans, and many Americans, will never forget:

Since this nation was founded...under God
More than 200 years ago
We have been the bastion of freedom
The light that keeps the free world aglow
We do not covet the possessions of others
We are blessed with the bounty we share.

We have rushed to help other nations
... anything...anytime...anywhere.

War is just not our nature
We won't start...but we will end the fight
If we are involved we shall be resolved
To protect what we know is right.

We have been challenged by a cowardly foe
Who strikes and then hides from our view.

With one voice we say, "There is no choice today,
There is only one thing to do.

Everyone is saying—the same thing—and praying
That we end these senseless moments we are living.

As our fathers did before...we shall win this unwanted war
And our children...will enjoy the future...we'll be giving."

As he reached the conclusion of his prose, Buck's voice cracked and his eyes watered. There wasn't a dry eye in the house. A 21-gun salute immediately followed Buck's reading and fireworks exploded over the stadium.

And so baseball resumed.

REMEMBERING JACK BUCK

So many who never met John Francis Buck knew him most of their lives.

They were Cardinals fans when Bob Gibson threw a no-hitter in 1971, when Lou Brock stole a 105th base in 1974, when Bruce Sutter struck out Gorman Thomas to end the 1982 World Series, when Ozzie Smith homered off Tom Niedenfuer in Game 5 of the 1985 National League Championship Series, when Jack Clark homered in Game 6, when Mark McGwire hit No. 62.

They were there when all of those things happened because Buck put them there, painted the picture, narrated the story.

Buck was born on August 21, 1924, in Holyoke, Massachusetts, the third of seven children to Earle and Kathleen Buck. In 1939, his father, a railroad accountant, moved the entire family to Cleveland, Ohio. Growing up, young Jack Buck became enchanted with baseball.

"Baseball was my great love," he said in his autobiography. "I listened to as many games and announcers as I could."

Earle Buck had managed a team in Erie, Pennsylvania, and even tried out for the New York Giants at one point. Likewise, his son Jack aspired to play professionally some day. But Earle Buck died at the age of 49 from uremic poisoning related to high blood pressure. Just 15 at the time, Jack Buck put his dreams aside and focused on helping support the family.

After graduating from high school, he worked on large freighters carrying iron ore in the Great Lakes. During that time, Buck applied for a promotion to the position of deck watch, but he didn't get it. A physical exam revealed he was colorblind, unable to see green and brown.

That probably comes as no surprise for Cardinals fans. They know Buck only saw Cardinals red.

The U.S. Army did not mind that Buck was colorblind and it drafted him in June 1943. Promoted to corporal, Buck was soon in the European theater, squad leader for a patrol that came under German fire in the Battle of Remagen. He sustained shrapnel wounds in his left forearm and leg and received the Purple Heart.

After shipping home in 1946, Buck attended Ohio State University, majoring in radio speech with a minor in Spanish. He began developing his radio skills by doing Ohio State basketball games. Upon graduation, Buck got a job doing play-by-play for the Cardinals' Class AAA affiliate in Columbus, Ohio, then spent a season calling games for the Rochester Red Wings of the International League.

In 1954, the Cardinals made Buck part of a broadcast team that included Harry Caray and Milo Hamilton. In 1959, the club dropped Buck to create an opening for Buddy Blattner, who had done St. Louis Browns games before the American League team moved to Baltimore. Blattner was also the voice of the NBA's St. Louis Hawks.

When Blattner departed in 1960, Buck was rehired, getting the job over Chick Hearn, who became a basketball institution with the Los

Angeles Lakers. A year later, Joe Garagiola departed the Cardinals' broadcast picture and Buck became the main sidekick for Caray for the next several seasons.

But in 1969, after 25 years of doing Cardinals games, Caray was fired. Stories circulated that Caray had been involved in an affair with Susan Busch, wife of August Busch III. Caray never denied the scuttlebutt, insisting the scurrilous talk was "good for my ego." He left St. Louis to work for the Oakland Athletics, then the Chicago White Sox, then the Chicago Cubs.

Buck became the lead play-by-play sound of the Cardinals for most of the next 30 years. When new partner Jim Woods left after one season, Buck was joined in the booth by former Cardinals player Mike Shannon in 1972. The two formed a 28-year union.

Buck also became widely regarded as a football broadcaster and began doing NFL games for CBS in 1964. In 1975, he briefly left his Cardinals duties to host an NBC pregame football show titled *GrandStand* alongside Bryant Gumbel. But Buck quickly returned.

From 1978 to 1996, he was the CBS radio voice of *Monday Night Football* with former coach Hank Stram as his partner. Buck's list of credits goes on and on, including everything from 17 Super Bowls to professional bowling. He was even the original play-by-play voice of the National Hockey League St. Louis Blues, describing all the action— or lack thereof—during the 1968 Stanley Cup Final. The Montreal Canadiens swept the Blues in four games.

In 1987, Buck was honored with the Ford Frick Award by the National Baseball Hall of Fame and Museum. In 1996, the football world followed suit and honored Buck with the Pete Rozelle Award at the Pro Football Hall of Fame in Canton, Ohio. "This is the first award I ever won where I didn't have to buy a table," Buck quipped.

In St. Louis, and over the vast areas of the Midwest that could pick up the 50,000-watt signal of KMOX Radio, Buck was the sound of

Cardinals baseball. His "that's a winner!" call after each Cardinals win became the soundtrack to warm summer days. Buck was also revered for his wit and personality as emcee and host of numerous awards dinners and charity functions in the community. In 1998, the Cardinals dedicated a bust outside the stadium to Buck, depicting him at the microphone, his hand cupped to one ear.

During the late 1990s, Buck's health deteriorated due to a series of conditions. He developed Parkinson's disease, diabetes, cataracts, sciatica, and vertigo, and had to use a pacemaker. The effects of Parkinson's became particularly noticeable late in his career, but he soldiered on. Hosting yet another awards dinner in 2000—and in typical Jack Buck style—he joked with the audience, "I wish I'd get Alzheimer's; then I could forget I've got all the other stuff."

Buck died at 11:08 PM on Tuesday, June 18, 2002, at Barnes-Jewish Hospital in St. Louis. He was 77 years old. He had been in the hospital since the beginning of the year, fighting lung cancer, infections, pneumonia, and the advance of other problems. His death shook the St. Louis community and inspired fans to leave flowers at the base of his bust outside the stadium throughout the night.

Flags at city and county government buildings were lowered to half-staff and local television anchors wore black suits for the next several days. A public visitation was held in the stadium before the next baseball game after his death, with free admission to the game for all the mourners who filed past his coffin.

"I wouldn't change a thing about my life," Buck wrote in a 1997 autobiography. "My childhood dreams came true."

And for Cardinals fans, Jack Buck brought so many more hopes and dreams to life.

Chapter 8

Things to Wear

Get a Cardinals Tattoo

Tattoos are associated with nearly every culture on earth. For instance, Otzi the Iceman, a 5,300-year-old mummy discovered in Europe in the 1990s, had more than 57 tattoos on his body. Many are believed to have been applied for therapeutic reasons, as a way of acupuncture or acupressure.

History reveals that many of our culture's most famous (or infamous) characters sported tattoos, including John F. Kennedy, Teddy Roosevelt, Winston Churchill, Thomas Edison, George Orwell, and John Wilkes Booth.

Body art certainly is prevalent today and still seems to be gaining in popularity. A 2014 Fox News poll showed that 20 percent of the U.S. voting population—or one in five—had at least one tattoo. That figure was up from 13 percent in 2007.

But there's more, literally and figuratively. The number of adults who acknowledged having more than one tattoo had nearly doubled in seven years, from 8 percent in '07 to 14 percent in 2014.

People under age 45 were twice as likely as the 45-and-over set to get tatted, and numbers went up as the ages went down. Thirty-four percent of the population under the age of 30 had ink, while one out of five in the age group had three or more tattoos.

Tattoo parlors sometimes charge a set fee. But they might also charge by the hour, a rate that can run anywhere from $60 to $250, depending on experience and skill level of the artist. If you're thinking of going the cheap route, review the aforementioned disclaimer about the "rest of your life." A good, full-sleeve tattoo can cost between $1,500 and $2,500. The other cost is the discomfort of having something carved into your body. The bigger the work, the bigger the pain.

With their affluent lifestyles, athletes tend to embrace the leading edge of cultural trends. At the same time, the warrior aspect of tattoos—which have always been popular with military personnel—makes ink all the more desirable.

To that end, the Cardinals have more than held their own in recent years. Catcher Yadier Molina has featured some of the more obvious displays, with tattoos on his neck clearly visible over his jersey and equipment. Molina doesn't chat about his tats, so he is not on record in explaining the art.

But the tattoo behind his left ear appears to be creative symbols for the first letters of his name, "Y" and "M." On the right side of his neck are musical notes in descending size and order. Tough to say exactly what they stand for—perhaps a special piece of music.

The native of Bayamon, Puerto Rico, keeps the ink peddlers busy. He also has Gold Gloves prominently displayed on his upper left arm. He has won the actual version for eight consecutive seasons through 2015. Last, but certainly not smallest, Molina has a giant tattoo of the

World Series trophy on his upper right arm. Listed are the years in which his Cardinals teams have won it: 2006 and 2011.

Another player with prominent paint is left fielder Matt Holliday. The Stillwater, Oklahoma, native has an elaborate cross imprinted on his right biceps, which he explains is "just sort of about my faith." More obvious is the Bible quote Holliday runs down the length of his left arm, starting at the base of his neck.

The long tattoo is from Job 38:4 and says, "Where were you when I laid the foundation of the earth? Tell me if you have understanding." Holliday explains, "It's just something that sort of puts me in my place."

He's not talking about left field.

Cardinals second baseman Kolten Wong has a full-sleeve tattoo that covers nearly all of his lower right arm. The native of Hilo, Hawaii, had the tattoo finished before coming to spring training in 2014. It is a tribute both to his Hawaiian heritage and to his mother, who died of cancer in December 2013.

The top part of Wong's arm was done first and is covered with patterns inspired by Hawaiian tribal symbols. Wong said the symbols represent his family, protection, and well being. On the underside of his forearm, stretching from just below his elbow to the wrist, is a ribbon crossing over, a symbol of cancer awareness and a remembrance of his mother.

"It's something I'm proud of," he said. "It means everything to me."

Cardinals third baseman Matt Carpenter has a tattoo under his right biceps that he had done when he was 21 years old. A native of Galveston, Texas, Carpenter was a junior at Texas Christian University at the time. He had gone unselected in the June baseball draft and to make matters worse, he had just blown out his right elbow. In short, his dreams of a career in baseball were floundering.

A day after having surgery on his elbow, Carpenter got the tattoo and he has been known as one of the hardest workers in the game ever since. His ink is a simple Bible-verse notation: Matthew 19:26. The actual verse reads, "With God all things are possible."

Carpenter explains, "I got that because at the time I didn't really know where I was going with my baseball career. I was in college and just wasn't on the right path that I thought I was going to go with my career. So it just meant I needed to put focus and hard work into what I was trying to do."

So, need a little inspiration? Need to be reminded, need to honor your favorite baseball team or player? Just remember, it won't mean a thing, if it ain't got that ink.

Doo-wa-doo-wa-doo-wa-doo-wa-doo-wa.

- -

Grow a Mustache Like Al Hrabosky

Alan Thomas Hrabosky remains one of the most colorful and memorable characters in Cardinals history. A first-round pick in the January 1969 amateur draft, the Oakland native and former Disneyland employee pitched for the Cardinals in parts of eight seasons (1970 to 1977).

Hrabosky was 40–20 with 59 saves as a Cardinal and 64–35 with 97 saves over his 13-year career, which included stops in Kansas City and Atlanta. Moreover, he developed a distinctive look, reputation, and shtick that left a lasting impression.

In 1974, with players like Reggie Jackson and Rollie Fingers having cracked the major league facial-hair barrier, Hrabosky decided he needed an edge. He embellished a 90-plus fastball with an unsettling appearance. Already blessed with heavy, dark eyebrows, the left-hander grew an equally thick mustache that dropped down and spread wider at the chin—a horseshoe on steroids, if you will.

To complement the look, he let his hair grow long and unkempt, flaring out the side of his cap. He then embraced a routine of self-motivation and intimidation that bordered on the absurd and caused quite the stir.

Between pitches, Hrabosky would turn and walk off the mound toward second base. Vigorously rubbing the ball, he would pause for a moment of self-reflection, then slam the baseball into his glove, spin around and stalk back to the top of the mound. He would menacingly kick aside dirt from the rubber, peer in for his sign, and scowl at the hitter like a homicidal maniac.

To further establish a malicious intent, Hrabosky had no qualms about uncoiling and sending his first fastball high and inside. In St. Louis, the crowd would roar with delight. In opposing cities, they would boo and heckle with disdain.

Opposing players did a little of both. "He gets you so mad he just whizzes the ball right by before you know it," said Chicago Cubs third baseman Bill Madlock, who initiated a bench-clearing brawl involving Hrabosky and catcher Ted Simmons in 1974. "I wish he was ours."

When it was working, Hrabosky's act was a thing of beauty. In 1974, a 24-year-old Hrabosky went 8–1 with 9 saves and 82 strikeouts in $88\frac{1}{3}$ innings. The following season, he was among the top closers in the National League, finishing 13–3 with a league-leading 22 saves and a 1.66 earned run average for a team that was a mediocre 82–80. He was third in the Cy Young voting and eighth in the voting for MVP, and named the *Sporting News* "Fireman of the Year."

These St. Louis friends admired Al Hrabosky's mustache so much that they founded the American Mustache Institute, or AMI. The group hosted its first event, "Stache Bash," at—where else—Hrabosky's Ballpark Saloon in St. Louis, which has since closed.

What's more, he had a new name. Cardinals public relations directors began referring to Hrabosky as the "Mad Hungarian," a nod to both his Hungarian heritage and his psychotic behavior. The name caught on with the press and with fans. Hrabosky even claimed to have developed a special pitch called the "Hungo," otherwise known as a forkball.

When Hrabosky wasn't selected to the National League team for the 1975 All-Star Game, the Cardinals held a "We Hlove Hrabosky Hbanner Hday" at the stadium during a game with the Dodgers and All-Star manager Walter Alston, the final series before the Summer

Classic break. Fans carrying a "We Hlove Hrabosky" banner were admitted free.

It was all great fun, until the Cardinals finished 72–90 in 1976. They fired manager Red Schoendienst and replaced him with St. Louis native Vern Rapp. On orders from ownership, the new skipper sought to establish a no-nonsense, disciplined environment. Before spring training, he wrote letters to all of his players, ordering them to cut their hair and get rid of any facial hair. This caused a rift between Rapp and several players, most notably Hrabosky and outfielder Bake McBride.

Initially, Hrabosky adhered to the policy and even ditched his "Mad Hungarian" routine. But during a game in early April, Dave Kingman hit a home run off Hrabosky and heckled him all the way around the bases. Incensed, Hrabosky went behind the mound, got himself properly enthused, and struck out the side to end the game.

A few weeks later, on a ABC Monday Night Baseball edition, he entered in the top of the ninth against the defending World Series champion Cincinnati Reds. With the game tied 5–5, he allowed the first three hitters (all left-handed) to reach, loading the bases with no outs.

As the Busch Stadium crowd went bananas, Hrabosky went into his "Mad Hungarian" act and proceeded to strike out right-handed sluggers George Foster, Johnny Bench, and Bob Bailey. An inning later, the Cardinals won the game on a Simmons home run.

But soon after, Hrabosky's relationship with Rapp came to a head and he was suspended indefinitely for refusing to meet with the manager. General Manager Bing Devine negotiated a truce and Hrabosky was reinstated two days later.

In July, owner Gussie Busch stepped in with a compromise. He lifted the ban on facial hair and extended Rapp's contract. In doing so, he read a statement that called out Hrabosky, who had complained that he was not himself without the menacing appearance.

"You said in the newspaper that you could only get batters out by being psyched up with your mustache and beard," Busch said. "Then go ahead and grow it. But, boy, are you going to look like a fool if you don't get the batters out...You painted me into a corner and no one does that to me."

Hrabosky got his hair back, but Camelot was over. Without the "Mad Hungarian" look, the southpaw had a mediocre 4.58 ERA in 37 games. After the amnesty, he was only marginally better, a 4.05 ERA in 28 games. All told, "Hungo" finished 6–5 with 10 saves and a 4.38 ERA.

Predictably, after the paint job on Busch, he was sent packing, traded at season's end to Kansas City for reliever Mark Littell and catcher Buck Martinez.

Rapp, whose unyielding approach got him in hot water in other areas, particularly when he called the well-respected Simmons a "loser," made it through a 83–79 season in '77. But when the team started 6–11 in 1978, he was also gone, replaced by former Cardinals star Ken Boyer.

Hrabosky remains a popular figure with the Cardinals, a member of the team's television broadcasting team and a frequent participant in fantasy camps and charitable events. Over the years, he has fluctuated in his shaving habits. But as of 2015, he was still rocking the Fu Manchu.

Own a Brockabrella

If you're a Cardinals fan, you know Lou Brock accomplished great things. He came to St. Louis by way of baseball's most famous trade—acquired from the Chicago Cubs for pitcher Ernie Broglio in a six-player deal in June 1964.

Broglio won a total of seven games as a Cub and was out of baseball altogether by 1967. Brock blossomed into a Hall of Fame Player in St. Louis and remained a Cardinal the rest of his career, sparking the team to three pennants and two World Series titles in the 1960s.

He became known as the Base Burgler and turned stealing bases into an art form. He broke the single-season record for stolen bases in 1974 and then shattered Ty Cobb's all-time major league stolen-bases mark in 1977.

He led the National League in stolen bases eight times and was an All-Star six times. He led the NL in doubles and triples in 1968, led the league in singles in 1972, and was a runner-up for the NL Most Valuable Player Award in 1974.

In 1985, he was inducted into the National Baseball Hall of Fame and he was part of the first class to be inducted into the St. Louis Cardinals Hall of Fame.

That's all impressive stuff, right? But perhaps Brock's most amazing accomplishment was to get people to buy and wear a Brockabrella. Whether Brock actually invented the product is a matter of debate. Upon seeing one, some might draw a conclusion that Inspector Gadget was somehow involved.

But the umbrella hybrid originally was distributed by Brock's St. Louis–based wholesale company, Brock World Products.

Regardless of who designated it, Brock certainly lent his name to the weird head gear that attaches to one's head and protects it from the elements. The Brockabrella was sold at ballparks with the idea that the strange-looking cap could be worn through games affected by showers. Rather than retreat to the concourse, fans could simply break out the Brockabrella and they were good to go.

And no, for those of you wondering, there was never a Brogliobrella that was traded to the Chicago market in return for the rights to the Brockabrella.

Odd as it is, the Brockabella became popular with Cardinals fans and gained somewhat of a cult audience around the country. In fact, under the category of "it takes one to know one," oddball outfielder Jay Johnstone was a fan. He was photographed wearing a Brockabella for his 1984 Fleer Chicago Cubs baseball card—talk about adding insult to injury.

The Brockabella still seems to pop up once in a while. In a game against Milwaukee in 2010, the Cardinals held a Brockabrella promotion at the ballpark, with the first 25,000 fans entering Busch Stadium receiving their very own Brockabrella.

Strangely, the Cardinals lost the game to the Brewers and the only stolen base was swiped by Milwaukee's Alcides Escobar.

So, while the Brockabrella is useful in keeping your head dry, and while it is an interesting piece of Cardinals history and pop culture, it may not be the best good-luck charm in the world.

If you can find a Cardinals-red blazer—Brooks Brothers makes the official Cardinals Hall of Fame one—you too could look like Lou Brock, Whitey Herzog, and Ted Simmons.

Add a Cardinals-Red Blazer to Your Wardrobe

Exclusive clubs often make use of a signature jacket to identify their members. Augusta National Golf Club might be the most obvious example. Members wear a green jacket, which is also presented annually to the winner of the Masters Tournament. He becomes an honorary member of the club, to go with the $1.8 million he takes home for winning the golf tournament. Thus, the green jacket is one of the most coveted prizes in sports.

But if you're a Cardinal, you might prefer a red one.

The Cardinals have adopted the jacket concept as part of their rich tradition. Beginning in the early 2000s, the club made it customary before home openers and postseason games to honor living members of the National Baseball Hall of Fame by introducing them wearing red blazers.

The original garment was a custom made two-button red jacket. The matching Brooks Brothers blazers were fashioned from 100% wool yarn in a sturdy weave, made to perform well all year long in St. Louis weather, which can be hotter than a Stan Musial line drive and as unpredictable as a Jaime Garcia start.

Each jacket featured the classic Cardinals birds-on-the-bat logo on the outside breast pocket, as well as an interior label bearing the Hall of Fame member's name, number, and year of induction.

In January 2014, the team expanded on the idea when chairman and chief executive officer William DeWitt Jr. announced plans for a formal Cardinals Hall of Fame induction process. A Red Ribbon committee of baseball experts was appointed to identify worthy candidates, and a six-week period of fan voting each spring elects those to be inducted during the Cardinals Hall of Fame enshrinement ceremony.

As part of that pomp and circumstance, each new member of the Cardinals Hall of Fame is presented with his very own red blazer to be worn at future Hall of Fame ceremonies, Opening Days, and other appropriate occasions.

The inaugural class was inducted in ceremonies at Ballpark Village in August 2014. Twenty-two members of the Cardinals already enshrined in the National Baseball Hall of Fame or honored with retired numbers were grandfathered in.

But the first Cardinals Hall of Fame class also featured four novice members voted in by fans, including former players Marty Marion, Jim Edmonds, and Willie McGee, and broadcaster Mike Shannon.

Each received a plaque on the wall at the Cardinals Hall of Fame Museum in Ballpark Village and the vaunted red blazer. Marion was represented by Martinna Dill, the oldest of his four daughters. Marion passed away in 2011.

During the induction ceremony, incumbent jacket wearers Lou Brock and Tony La Russa helped Edmonds put on his new attire.

"This is beyond belief to put on the red jacket," Edmonds said. "I was a little confused at first about the red jacket, didn't know if I'd ever get to wear it. Now, I'm not sure I'm worthy of it."

Edmonds had the perspective of watching the likes of Brock, Stan Musial, Bob Gibson, Ozzie Smith, and Red Schoendienst wear the red blazers many times during his eight seasons in St. Louis. He never contemplated the idea that he might be fitted.

"That's been the hardest part, to kind of figure how to deal with that from watching those guys from a distance for the last 12–14 years," said Edmonds, who won six Gold Gloves and played in six postseasons with the organization. "When they told me I was getting a red jacket, I had to step back a little bit. I think this red jacket symbolizes much more than a plaque on the wall."

Edmonds played the jacket forward when he slipped it on Ted Simmons during the 2015 ceremony. Simmons was inducted along with Curt Flood, Bob Forsch, and George Kissell. The former Cardinals catcher explained how special it was by saying only four franchises in baseball—the Dodgers, Giants, Yankees, and Cardinals—have such pedigree.

"They've got all the Hall of Famers and all the pennants. Those four places are huge," Simmons said.

"When one of them, in this case, the Cardinals, embraces you, brings you forward and lifts you up, along with their fan base, which says, 'We really think there's something special about you'…it was a little surprising the way people got vocal like they did....You can't ignore it. This really has been a special day."

To be clear, the new Cardinals Hall of Fame jacket is not exactly the same as the garment the Cooperstown Cardinals originally wore. For one, the members who also have been inducted into the National Baseball Hall of Fame wear an HOF pin from Cooperstown that is not worn by the Cardinals HOFers.

What's more, Brooks Brothers was not able to match the original red blazer they provided to Musial, Gibson, Brock, Smith, and others. The company had to use a different dye lot for the Cardinals Hall of Fame blazers and a slightly different material. Both the original dye and original material were no longer made.

La Russa is now chief of baseball operations for the Arizona Diamondbacks. His current team played at San Diego on April 13, 2015, the same day as the Cardinals' home opener in St. Louis. La Russa was so excited and respectful of the opportunity to wear the red blazer and take his place among the Hall of Fame inductees, he took part in the ceremonies at Busch Stadium, even as a member of an opposing team. He was able to catch a flight the same afternoon and make it to the Diamondbacks game with the Padres that night.

"Are you kidding? I wouldn't miss it," La Russa said. "I have too much respect for this organization and these fans."

Perhaps Ozzie Smith says it best when it comes to the wearin' o' the two-button red.

"I've always said the business we're in is the business of creating memories, creating memories that last a lifetime," Smith explained. "That red jacket means something special here, something you can't put into words, something that lasts a lifetime.

"Baseball is like a religion in St. Louis. The people are weaned on it from day one. Once a Cardinal fan, always a Cardinal fan."

Once in a red jacket, always in a red jacket.

Checklist

CHECKLIST

Things to Do

☐ Throw Out the First Pitch at a Cardinals Game
☐ Frame the Classic 1968 *Sports Illustrated* Magazine Cover
☐ Name a Child or Pet "Vinegar Bend"
☐ Play St. Louis Cardinals Monopoly
☐ Roll the Dice on "First Pitch" Tickets
☐ Attend Cardinals Fantasy Camp
☐ Ride the Redbird Express
☐ Cross the Stan Musial Bridge and Visit Donora, Pennsylvania
☐ Cruise with the Cardinals
☐ Get Opening Day in St. Louis Declared a Civic Holiday
☐ Get Over 1985
☐ Forgive Don Denkinger
☐ Catch a Souvenir Ball at a Cardinals Game
☐ Get Beaked by Fredbird
☐ Settle the Feud between Tony La Russa and Ozzie Smith
☐ Own a 1994 Fleer Pro-Visions No. 5 Ozzie Smith Baseball Card
☐ Join Redbird Nation
☐ Purchase a Personalized Brick at Busch Stadium
☐ Donate to Cardinals Care

Things to Read

☐ Read *A Well-Paid Slave: Curt Flood's Fight for Free Agency in Professional Sports*
☐ Read *October 1964* by David Halberstam
☐ Read Bob Gibson's *Stranger to the Game*
☐ Read Tony La Russa's Books

Places to Go

☐ Attend Cardinals Spring Training
☐ Meet Someone at the Stan Musial Statue
☐ Visit the Real Stan Musial Statue in Springfield, Missouri
☐ Visit Ballpark Village

- [ ] Visit the Cardinals Hall of Fame Museum
- [ ] Sit in the Cardinals Club Seats for a Game
- [ ] Visit Grant's Farm
- [ ] Attend the St. Louis Baseball Writers Awards Dinner
- [ ] See a Cards–Cubs Game at Wrigley Field

Places to Eat
- [ ] Eat at Soup's Sports Grill
- [ ] Eat at Harry Caray's Restaurant
- [ ] Eat at Mike Shannon's Steaks and Seafood

Things to See
- [ ] Experience Opening Day in St. Louis
- [ ] See a Game at AutoZone Park in Memphis
- [ ] See Cardinals Exhibits at the National Baseball Hall of Fame and Museum in Cooperstown
- [ ] Watch *The Pride of St. Louis*
- [ ] See a Springfield Cardinals Texas League Game in Springfield, Missouri
- [ ] Take a Busch Stadium Tour and See Trinket City
- [ ] Witness a Cardinals No-Hitter

Things to Know
- [ ] Learn to Play "Take Me Out to the Ball Game" on the Harmonica
- [ ] Learn to Score the Cardinal Way
- [ ] Learn to Do an Ozzie Smith Backflip

Things to Hear
- [ ] Listen to Sam Bush's Song "The Wizard of Oz"
- [ ] Hear Bob Costas Refer to Ozzie Smith as a Power Hitter
- [ ] Hear Ozzie Smith Sing "Cupid"
- [ ] Hear Jack Buck's 9/11 Poem

Things to Wear
- [ ] Get a Cardinals Tattoo
- [ ] Grow a Mustache Like Al Hrabosky
- [ ] Own a Brockabrella
- [ ] Add a Cardinals-Red Blazer to Your Wardrobe

Appendix

WORLD SERIES TITLES

2011

2006 • 1982

1967 • 1964

1946 • 1944

1942 • 1934

1931 • 1926